LAST OF THE LINE

LAST OF THE LINE

PATRICIA GUMBRELL

Whittles Publishing

Published by
Whittles Publishing,
Dunbeath Mains Cottages,
Dunbeath,
Caithness KW6 6EY,
Scotland, UK
www.whittlespublishing.com

Typeset by
Samantha Barden

© 2005 P. M. Gumbrell

ISBN 1-904445-12-8

Printed in the UK by
Athenaeum Press Ltd., Gateshead, Tyne & Wear

Contents

Introduction

Without fail, the lighthouses and beacons around our coasts will shine out for the protection and safety of mariners sailing around our coasts. Now that the era of automation is with us, the human time and effort given in the past to perform these tasks should not be forgotten.

The author, Patricia Madge Gumbrell, was born on 27th August 1937 to Josephine Mary and Harold Owen Hall. After two years of temporary service Harold Hall entered permanent service with the Corporation of Trinity House in May 1922 and retired in September 1966 having served in many of the lighthouses around the coast. Upon his retirement he recorded the experiences of his ancestors and memories of his childhood and service as a lighthouse keeper.

In this book memories and stories of 200 years of lighthouse keeping are related, from three families connected by marriage. Since the author accompanied her parents to the locations where her father was posted, her own experiences of conditions as a lightkeeper's daughter are vividly recalled also. Now that there are no keepers manning the lighthouses around our coast, this account will serve as an important reminder to a way of life not seen today.

David Gumbrell

A painting of Bishop Rock lighthouse by my father, Harold Hall.
Courtesy of Comet newspaper, North Hertfordshire.

1

The Corporation of Trinity House

The story begins at a small village called Dale on the Pembrokeshire coast. Henry Tudor landed close by in a cove called Mill Bay on 7th August 1485 with his followers to start on an expedition that would lead to the battle of Bosworth, and then on to his coronation as King Henry VII of England. It was in 1514 that Henry VIII granted a charter to 'The Master, Wardens and Assistants of the Guild or Fraternity of the Most Glorious and Undividible Trinity of St Clement in the Parish of Deptford Strond' to regulate pilotage around his realm. From here this grew to be the Corporation of Trinity House of today, with its Master HRH The Prince Philip, Duke of Edinburgh and a Deputy Master as Executive Chairman and board of 'Elder Brethren'. These Elder Brethren are drawn from a group of experienced Royal Navy and Merchant Service sea officers who are elected as 'Younger Brethren'.

Dale had been a thriving port in Elizabethan times and much coastal trading took place there, but it fell to decline as ships became larger in the 18th century. Coastal trading continued at a lesser rate throughout the 19th and early 20th centuries, transporting the heavy commercial goods that would otherwise have been difficult.

Thomas Hall, of whom I am the sixth generation granddaughter, also arrived in Dale and also contributed, through many years of service, to the history of coastal navigation. Originating from the northeast of England, he was baptised in 1734 and became the husband of Margaret Mussavin of Flemish origin in 1760. He was a mariner and had a large family. Three of his sons also became mariners but the youngest of these, John Hall, unfortunately drowned at sea in 1810. This happened a few weeks before the birth of John's own son, also named John.

In November 1816 John Hall's widow married again, to a boat owner. Her son John's childhood days were very happy, and perhaps a great fuss was made of him, as he had four older sisters Sarah, Mary, Elizabeth and Margaret. He showed early signs of talent and it was thought he inherited this from his grandmother Margaret. John became an expert at handling his stepfather's boats, and to the dismay of his mother seemed to be inclined to follow a calling of the sea like his father and grandfather Thomas Hall before him. She was therefore relieved when he commenced duties as a lightkeeper, perhaps inspired by his brother-in-law Richard Lloyd or his uncle William Warlow, both lightkeepers. John was appointed to St Ann's Head, close to Dale. He married Elizabeth Jones in 1831 and together they had seven children.

John Hall with his wife Elizabeth and their son, Thomas Owen Hall.

St Ann's is the oldest established lighthouse on the Welsh coast, approved by Trinity House in 1662. At one time two lights were exhibited at St Ann's from two towers 610 feet apart, but the second tower was rebuilt in 1844. In 1877 a fog signal was established. Since 1910, only the modern light has been in use.

Shortly after 1841 John requested a transfer to the Skerries lighthouse, situated off Anglesey north of Holyhead. Established in 1717, Skerries was one of the last private lighthouses to be acquired by Trinity House about the time John was made Principal there.

Although the charter from Henry VIII gave Trinity House the authority to regulate navigation around the coast, they did not at first build or own all lighthouses. Individuals with a particular interest would often obtain permission and license to build and operate a lighthouse. Since they were allowed to collect dues from shipping, operating a lighthouse would in most cases be very profitable. It was not until 1836 that an Act of Parliament empowered Trinity House to acquire and manage all lighthouses around the coast.

It was at the Skerries that a young Henry Thomas Knott was appointed as an assistant keeper in 1875. Henry was the fifth generation to follow the tradition of the Knotts as lightkeepers. His father George Knott served as Principal Keeper at the Eddystone's third tower, built by John Smeaton in 1795. It was eventually dismantled, brought ashore and rebuilt on Plymouth Hoe. The fourth and existing tower was built by Sir James Douglass in 1882. Henry had assisted his father at Bideford Bar Lights in North Devon and at Bull Point lighthouse near Ilfracombe. When his father was stationed at the Eddystone lighthouse situated about 12 miles off Plymouth he was apprenticed as a shipwright in what was then known as Plymouth Dock. When he had finished his apprenticeship he joined the service of Trinity House.

George Knott with his model of North Foreland lighthouse.

From the Skerries, Henry would make occasional trips to the shore in a small boat to collect food and mail. He would take letters to the rented home of the Principal Keeper John Hall in Holyhead. Here he would see John Hall's daughter Ellen Margaret. After a courtship that lasted about two years they were married in St Seriol's Church, Holyhead, on 3rd December 1877. Henry and Ellen Margaret had five children, the youngest two being twins. Shortly after the birth of the twins in January 1886 their mother Ellen Margaret died of pneumonia.

John Hall retired in Holyhead after serving for almost fifty years. Only three of the seven children of his marriage survived into adulthood. His son Thomas Owen was to continue in the service of Trinity House, serving in the sailing cutter until he transferred to lighthouses in 1860. When John died in 1881, Thomas Owen was by then the Principal at Inner Farne Light, having been appointed there in 1862 after two years as a Supernumerary Assistant Keeper. He had also served at stations such as Eddystone and Bishop Rock Light.

Eddystone lighthouse, 12 miles off the coast of Plymouth. Photograph courtesy of Christopher Nicholson.

My great grandfather Thomas Owen Hall.

2

The Darling Connection: Farne Islands

It was at the Farne Islands that my great grandfather Thomas Owen Hall met and married my great grandmother Grace Horsley Darling. She had been named after her aunt who had been made famous by the 1838 rescue of the survivors of the SS *Forfarshire*, carried out with her father William Darling.

My great grandmother Grace Horsley Darling, named after her aunt.

The Darling family had been associated with the lighthouses on the Farne Islands, a 'black spot' for shipping, since 1795. William Darling's journal records over 110 shipwrecks at the islands between 1795 and 1860 as well as the part he and his family played in helping to save people from some of those wrecks.

The Farne Islands are situated off the east coast of England between the towns of Bamburgh and Seahouses in the county of Northumberland. Their proximity to the coast (ranging from two to four miles) means they represent a serious hazard to shipping. To attempt to reduce the hazards, lighthouses were established from as early as 1776 on the Inner Farne Islands but replaced later by two towers in 1810 that were mainly to aid inshore traffic. In 1826 a lighthouse was built on the Longstone Island, although dangers extend over three-quarters of a mile to the northeast of this location. Earlier than this, a lighthouse on Staple Island had suffered from weather damage. A further lighthouse established on the Brownsman Island was considered inadequate and discontinued.

My great grandmother related many stories of the Darling family and their association with the Farne Islands and Coquet Island (twenty miles south of the Farnes) to my father. She told of her great grandfather Robert Darling, and his six sisters. Their father was a Presbyterian Minister and they lived north of the border in Duns, Scotland. At the age of twenty in 1769, Robert settled in the village of Belford in Northumberland, worked as a cooper, and courted and married Elizabeth Clark. They had eight children, the youngest named William who was born in 1786. Robert was given the responsible task of keeping the beacon lit at Brownsman Island in 1795, the beginning of the Darling family's history at the Farne islands. His son William attended the school at Bamburgh for a while, but by 1799 he was assisting his father at his lightkeeping tasks.

Robert was aware of the terrible toll in lives and ships which the Farnes had seen in the eighteenth century when over fifty ships were wrecked, but he could not have foreseen that he and his family would save so many lives in their small boat. For example, within just a few months of commencing duties, the sloop *Friendship* struck the west side of Brownsman, and although he managed to save two exhausted men, four were drowned. Almost five years later the galliot *Maxmilian Frederick* struck Longstone, and although one seaman drowned Robert managed to save eight others. In 1802, the schooner *Caledonia* struck Longstone, and Robert together with William managed to save four lives.

His beacon was situated about four miles east-northeast of Bamburgh Castle and surrounded by dangerous rocks. Although the rocks were in many cases only exposed during low water, Robert and William knew them well. The names of all the rocks were known by heart to all who lived there, and were constantly used in conversation. For example, any member of the family could go and haul in crab pots if they had been told only the name of the nearest rock or scar. A mile east of their beacon was a group of rocks known as the Crumstone, of which one was named the Fang rock. To the northeast were the Longstone rocks with the treacherous Knivestone rock. In between Brownsman and Longstone were the Harcar rocks, upon which the ill-fated steamship *Forfarshire* was wrecked in 1838. To the northwest were the Wamses, about a mile west were the Elbow, Megstone, and Swedman rocks, and to the southwest was the Solan rock.

William Darling, whose father Robert began the Darling history at the Farne Islands in 1795.

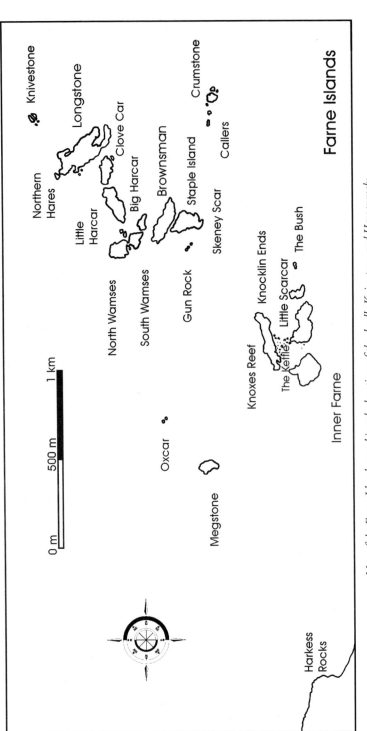

Knivestone

Longstone

Clove Car

Northern
Hares

Little
Harcar

Big Harcar

Brownsman

Staple Island

Crumstone

Callers

Skeney Scar

Gun Rock

North Wamses

South Wamses

Knocklin Ends

The Bush

Little Scarcar

The Kettle

Knoxes Reef

Oxcar

Megstone

Inner Farne

Harkess
Rocks

0 m   500 m   1 km

Farne Islands

Map of the Farne Islands, marking the locations of the deadly Knivestone and Harcar rocks.

The family lived in a stone cottage, where their mornings were occupied by hauling the fuel up to the top of the tower for the night's burning. They also spent many hours in the huge gardens, where they grew all their requirements such as corn, maize and vegetables, and in building walls to protect the gardens from the northeast gales. William spent a very happy life at Brownsman, because although he had to share the night watches with his father, taking his turn to stoke the Brazier as a warning to the mariner, he enjoyed many other pastimes such as fishing, catching rabbits, or collecting bird's eggs.

William married Thomasina Horsley on 1st July 1805, a member of one of the oldest local families. His new wife was a descendent of Roger de Horsley, a former Constable of Bamburgh Castle and landowner as far back as 1332. They lived on Brownsman in the cottage that he and his father had extended. On 6th April 1806 the first child of the marriage was born and named William, followed two years later on 7th August 1808 by twins named Thomasina and Mary Ann.

In 1809, Trinity House completed the building of a lighthouse at Inner Farne Island, equipped with a revolving light consisting of oil burning Argand lamps with reflectors. A similar tower was built at Brownsman in 1810. The night watches were found to be less arduous than previous and Trinity House journals were introduced. These required the signature of each watchman, the duration of his watch, temperature and barometric readings and the completion of a remarks column by the senior keeper to include any event considered of importance.

On 30th December 1810, just after the establishment of the revolving light, the fourth child of William and Thomasina was born, named Job Horsley. Their fifth was named Elizabeth, born in Bamburgh on 15th August 1812. This was followed a year later, almost to the day, by the death of Robert's wife Elizabeth, who was taken ashore for burial at Belford. The sixth child of William and Thomasina was born on Brownsman on 29th March 1814, the weather being too severe to allow the boat trip to Bamburgh. He was named Robert after his Grandfather who, unfortunately, had begun to fail in health from the moment that his wife died and only survived her by twenty months.

William took over where his father had left off, assisted by his wife and family. Their eldest son William, now only nine years old, was equivalent to a fifteen-year-old in stature, and was just as fearless in the boat as his ancestors had been. In August 1815, the sloop *Sarah*, bound from Leith to

London struck the Knivestone rock. Fortunately they managed to save all hands, bringing them to the Brownsman from where they were later taken to the mainland by local fishermen.

William's wife Thomasina was not very fond of the boat, so he took advantage of a calm day to ensure that she would be in good hands at Bamburgh in plenty of time for an expected event, and on 24th November 1815, their seventh child Grace Horsley Darling was born in a cottage which has since been visited by thousands. Grace was destined to become a national heroine, by helping her father to save nine lives. More importantly however, was the fact that her action led to a public demand for more stringent regulations to ensure the safety of those at sea.

The Knivestone rock, the most dreaded in the group, was invisible at high water, and two attempts to erect a beacon on it failed. The first in June 1816 lasted only six months, and the second, completed in July 1818, was washed away after fifteen months. Shortly after the first beacon on the Knivestone was destroyed, the brig *Hero* struck the same rock and became a total loss. On this occasion, four fishermen from Seahouses also assisted at the wreck, but the weather was so severe that they and eight members of the crew had to remain at Brownsman for over a week before the weather moderated.

On 14th August 1819, Thomasina gave birth to twin boys on the Brownsman named George Alexander and William Brookes. Four days after this event, the smack *Hope* of Leith on passage to London ran aground. The passengers and crew had to remain at Brownsman until the weather improved.

On 2nd February 1823, a very severe blizzard struck the islands, and William and his family witnessed the total loss with all hands of the *George and Mary*, the *Fortitude* and the *Augusta*. Two months later, a schooner named the *Undate* struck the Knivestone and was lost, although William found the crew on the Longstone rock the next morning. It was at this time that Trinity House decided to build the Longstone Lighthouse, which was lit for the first time on 15th February 1826. The Brownsman light was then extinguished.

William moved his family and furniture to Longstone although they could not cut their ties with Brownsman. Each day, weather permitting, trips were made in order to attend to the gardens, catch rabbits, or collect eggs. He had been given permission to make full use of the amenities there. No time was wasted in bad weather however, as he would use the lantern as a schoolroom and set lessons for his children while keeping a constant vigil. My great grandmother said, "If it taught nothing else, besides the three R's, it certainly instilled common sense into them". She was speaking from personal experience, as she was tutored by her father at the Coquet Island when she lived there, and later by her Grandfather, William Darling Senior, at Longstone.

Visiting Longstone lighthouse with my grandchildren Laurie and Millie.

Six years after the completion of the Longstone tower the schooner *Sisters of Newcastle* was wrecked on the south Bluecap. William and his eldest son managed to save the crew. Two years later, in December 1834, the sloop *Autumn* struck the Knivestone and sank almost immediately. Only one survivor was saved.

The story of Grace Darling and the ill-fated journey of the paddle steamer *Forfarshire*, which struck the Harcars rocks in the early hours of 7th September 1838, need hardly be repeated. However, my great grandmother had spent many hours in the boat fishing with her grandfather William Darling Senior, over the same route he had taken with his daughter Grace, and the story as he related it to my great grandmother went:

"We had a gale from the east the day before, and just before midnight, Gracie and I had to put everything into the tower, make the boat fast on the stand, and she kept the light until three o'clock, when she called your grandmother. They both shook me at five, and told me they could see something on the Harcar, so I took the big glass up, and sure enough, we could see the paddle box of a ship, and some people on the rocks, so after having a hot drink, we launched the boat, leaving your grandmother to put the light out. If your Aunt Gracie had put on another shawl, and worn a bonnet, I think she would be alive today.

"The sea was much smoother behind the Harcar, where we found eight men and a woman named Dawson, who was very distressed because her two children had died from the cold during the night, and we pulled to the Longstone end, landing your aunt, who took Mrs Dawson and two of the men to the tower. Two of the men rowed back with me to get the four who had stayed behind, and by nine o'clock we were all at home having a hot drink, but as soon as I could I took the glass up top because I knew that your Uncle Brookes would have seen what was happening, and sure enough, I could see them coming out of Seahouses harbour in one of the big cobles, landing at Harcar, and then pulling over to the Longstone end when they saw us walking along. It was still blowing hard but as there were enough of us we carried their boat along and lashed it down near the tower where it had to stay for a few days.

"Your Aunt Gracie was only twenty seven when she died, on 20th October 1842, a year before you were born, and she loved the Coquet, where she was staying when she became ill, and your Father took her to Alnwick, where she had all the medical care and attention possible".

My great grandmother spent her childhood at Coquet Island, as her father William (the brother of Grace), the eldest son of William Darling Senior, was the first keeper at the lighthouse established in 1841. She remembered, "In the late summer of 1859, we were packing our furniture at Coquet, all ready to go to the Longstone. Our place had been taken at Coquet by Uncle William Brookes, who arrived a few days before we left, and we had great fun with the weather being grand. When we arrived at Longstone, we lived in the cottage beside the tower that had been built for Uncle William Brookes. When Grandfather retired in October 1860, Father took his place so we moved into the tower and an assistant keeper, Mr Dyer, came to live in the cottage. Our first winter was very bad, and in the month of March, a brig named the *Florence Nightingale* struck the Knivestone rock and broke up. Father and two of your Great Uncles went out in the boat, but Grandfather insisted on going as well, but he retired seven months later".

Coquet lighthouse, where my great grandmother spent her childhood

A few weeks before William Darling Senior retired, the sloop *Trio* from Arbroath drove on to the Harcars in the same spot that the *Forfarshire* had struck. It was blowing so hard that it was after tea time before they could bring the two survivors in, and one of them was in very bad shape. The next day the signal was put up for the tender, which came out and took them to Seahouses. Aunt Thomasina and cousin Georgian went to live in Bamburgh with William Senior when he retired, and in 1864 my great grandmother Grace Darling married my great grandfather Thomas Owen Hall, keeper at Inner Farne. William Darling Junior, my great grandmother's father, died on duty at the Longstone on 6th November 1869 at the age of sixty-three, only surviving his father by four years.

My great grandmother was sixteen years old when she left Coquet and was eighteen when my great grandfather arrived at the Farne islands. My father asked her on one occasion how they managed to do their courting. "Sometimes he would come off to Longstone, sometimes Father and I would pull to Inner Farne, and when the weather was fine, we could pull to Brownsman!" was her amused reply.

Grace and Thomas Owen had five children: Elizabeth in 1867, my grandfather John William in 1870, Tom in 1876, Robert in 1879, and William in 1882. The family had a huge collection of books at Inner Farne, some of which Thomas Owen had brought over from Holyhead when they married and some from Grace's father who had been given them by his sister Grace.

My grandfather John William Hall has related many stories and experiences of life on Farne Island to my father Harold Owen Hall. He said, "We made full use of the books at Inner Farne, and we were somewhat of a headache to the teachers, because we were always in classes with much older children, being able to read and write at the age of four.

"Before we went to live in North Sunderland, we used to pray for rough weather each Monday, in order that we could spend more time at the island, where we each had our own particular job to do, taking turns in cleaning St Cuthbert's Chapel, the dwellings, the gardens and the donkey's stable.

"The donkey was almost human, and was known locally because of his liking for a special brand of beer. We could not catch him if the weather was calm enough for a boatload of visitors to land, as no boat landed without bringing a few bottles. They were all highly amused to see the donkey, holding a bottle between crossed forelegs, unscrewing the cork, firmly holding the neck between the teeth, and then tipping its head back until the bottle was empty. Sometimes the donkey was a bit unsteady in his walk, and Father used to step in, but I don't know if he was concerned so much about the donkey, or whether he thought there was a lot of good beer being wasted.

"When I was eighteen, in 1889, the Trinity House painters arrived to paint Inner Farne lighthouse and dwellings. As they were short handed the foreman took me on, and I liked it so much that I was with them for three years. After we finished Inner Farne, we painted Longstone, Coquet Island, Belle Toute (the old Beachy Head light), the Usk lighthouses in Monmouthshire, Bardsey Island, Skerries light, South Stack, and Menai light in Anglesey, and I joined the service as a Supernumerary Assistant Keeper in April, 1892."

Inner Farne lighthouse, where my grandfather John Hall grew up. Photograph courtesy of Christopher Nicholson.

3

The First World War: Coquet Lighthouse

By the time my grandfather, John William Hall, had joined the Trinity House service in 1892, his own father Thomas Owen had been transferred to the Flamborough lighthouse further south down the coast. It was here that he died while on duty in 1899 and his wife Grace then went to live with her daughter Elizabeth Ann in Hull.

Flamborough lighthouse, where my great grandfather died while on duty in 1899.
Photograph courtesy of Christopher Nicholson.

John William spent his two years as Supernumerary Assistant Keeper (SAK) stationed at Happisburgh Norfolk, Souter Point off the Tyne, Bishop

Rock off the Isles of Scilly and Hurst Castle at the entrance of the Solent. In 1894, he was promoted to Assistant Keeper at the Wolf Rock Light off Lands End. It was in Cornwall that he met my grandmother Ann Pascoe, who came from Helston. They were married in 1896 at the Church of St Mary the Virgin in Penzance. He was transferred to South Foreland lighthouse in 1897, where Guglielmo Marconi, the pioneer of wireless telegraphy visited, whom John William often assisted with his experiments.

Wolf Rock lighthouse, where my grandfather was first promoted to Assistant Keeper.
Photograph courtesy of Christopher Nicholson.

My grandparents, John and Anne Hall.

Sadly, in 1902, two lightkeepers were drowned at Dovercourt High and Low Lights near Harwich. John William was one of the keepers sent to replace them. My father, Harold Owen, was born at Dovercourt and it was here that he spent most of a happy boyhood. He remembered having a blackboard and chalk when he was only four years old, and with help from his father, he could read and write before he began school. School days at Dovercourt were happy for him, and after school he would run errands for his mother or go to the beach to sail his model yacht.

He and his brother were choristers at St Augustine's Church and they witnessed the church parades from the Ganges training ship for the Royal Navy, afloat at Shotley. The children of the area were always excited when the German Brass Bands visited from the Hook of Holland to play in the streets. In 1907 there was very little traffic on the roads with the exception of the occasional horse-drawn vehicle. They also saw the Hungarians with their performing bears, the travelling people with their knife-grinding machines, and the carts that displayed rows of swinging kettles and a colourful selection of paper windmills. He remembered the arrival of the first seaplane at Harwich, brought in by Commander Samson. He would look forward to weekends when his father's friend would allow Harold to row him to his yacht that was moored in the Bay or even go sailing with him and his visitors.

My father was still a schoolboy at the outbreak of the First World War in 1914, which was shortly after his father John William was promoted to Principal Keeper at the Coquet Lighthouse. This was fifty-five years after his mother Grace and her father William Darling Junior had left there to go to the Longstone Lighthouse.

The move to Coquet was delayed by bad weather and the family had to stay with relations in Amble, so my father and his sisters began attending school there. His elder brother Thomas Edwin, who had started serving his time as a fitter in Dovercourt, was anxious to continue at the school, so it was arranged for him to live with his uncle in Bradford. He was soon employed in a munitions factory, but in 1916 he joined the Seaforth Highlanders by adding a year to his age.

My father was given his schoolwork to take to Coquet, but his sisters stayed on the mainland and were brought back for the weekends. In spite of the war, my father had a happy life at Coquet. His first job each day was to milk the goats, and he did not need an alarm clock as the goats would begin braying at sunrise. (He claimed the goats could sense if something unusual was happening. For example, if the boat was launched to go to the mainland they would follow the party to the boat and would be waiting on the beach for their return, but never displayed this curiosity when the boat was launched simply for some fishing.)

After milking the goats, my father's next job was to make a complete circuit of the island and to put above the high water mark any timber that might have been washed ashore during the night. If the tide was low enough he would also remove any lobsters or crabs from the pots in the deeper pools, and put them in an anchored store box. Gardening followed, depending on the weather, and two hours of each afternoon were reserved for schoolwork.

At half tide, half an hour would be all that was required for rod fishing at his favourite spot on the west side of the island. Alternatively, at low water spring tides, he would spear some good-sized plaice in what the family named the Lagoon. The Lagoon only formed at dead low water on spring tides, so the fishing had to be quick and before he had mastered the art of spearing them, he lost plenty in a flurry of sandy cloudy water. He learnt to approach them from behind when they were lying on the bottom, and to direct his spear not at the plaice but in front.

There were other tasks, such as salting fish, drying them in the sun or smoking them over a slow burning oak fire. There were also rabbits to be caught and sea bird's eggs (chiefly Eider ducks eggs) to be collected if they had been laid below high water mark. He remembered the first summer in 1915, when he told his father that he had seen an Eider duck's nest with eggs in it. His father said, "Don't touch them, there will be plenty of rogue's eggs". His father was right, and after showing him where to look with the telescope, he could retrieve quite a number of eggs that had been laid on the bare rock below high water mark.

All navigation buoys in the vicinity of Coquet existed in duplicate, one set moored and the other set housed in the buoy store on the island, swapped over and repainted every twelve months. My father's first job when these were brought in was to scrape off all the tiny mussels growing on the mooring shackles and place them in what was called the bait pool, where they would soon grow large enough to be used for pollock fishing. After each buoy had been repainted, he took great pride in the job of painting the name on each buoy.

As well as pleasant memories of daily life, my father also recalled a dramatic event during the winter of 1915-1916. Due to persistent northeast gales the lighthouse families were on the verge of starvation, having been unable to make their weekly shopping trip to the port of Amble for several weeks. Their means of contact was a small boat of the type known on the northeast coast as a coble, which could be handled by two men although my father always assisted enabling the third oar to be used. When at last the eagerly awaited calm morning arrived, it was hardly necessary for the morning watchman to shout out, "Fit for boat work". In fact, everyone was already busy adding to the long list of required supplies and ensuring that all letters had been placed in the watertight mailbag. They set off in high spirits for Amble harbour at 09:30.

Since there was no wind that morning, they had to pull all the way, their view over the stern being a constant reminder that there was a shortage of food on the island. Crossing the harbour bar, they realised to their dismay that a ground swell was starting up. By the time they had moored their boat, huge seas were breaking across the harbour mouth, leaving several fishing cobles outside in need of assistance. A chartered naval tug steamed out and towed these in, each boat having filled up to the thwarts with seawater. It was obvious that if they had set off twenty minutes later, they too would have been in need of assistance. By this time they were most anxious because although the Commander of the naval tug had offered to tow them back to the island, the Harbour Master had closed the port for all outward-bound traffic. John William requested instructions by telephone, and was advised by Trinity House to make every effort to return to the lighthouse without running any undue risk to life, and if all other means failed, he was authorised to call upon the help of the nearest lifeboat. After discussing the situation with the assistant keeper, he decided to contact the Hauxley lifeboat station. He asked the coxswain of the *Mary Andrews* if enough volunteers could be found and was told, "Every man, woman and child is willing to help".

John William and his assistant decided that my father should be left onshore, much to his disappointment. Since he considered himself a member of the boat crew he argued and pleaded until they agreed he could accompany them. The main bulk of the stores had to be left on the mainland but having gathered up as many parcels of food as they could carry, they set off on a two-mile walk to the village of Hauxley. On arrival, they found that the inhabitants were enthusiastically at work, pulling the lifeboat *Mary Andrews* out of the boathouse. They were touched at the sight of such a large crowd.

Having placed their parcels in the lifeboat, they all grabbed the towing ropes of the lifeboat carriage and within a few minutes arrived at the beach. The coxswain decided however, that it would be unwise to launch the lifeboat at that particular spot as the beach sloped too steeply. One mile further north in Whitehouse Bay the slope towards the sea was more gradual which meant that the waves would break further out and would have lost their momentum before reaching the shore.

Their spirits were lifting at this stage because they knew that my grandmother would be able to see that some action was being taken. The coast guards had been requested not to make a semaphore signal as she had not enough experience in reading it, and it would simply have provided additional anxiety. Even with their lighter moods and the assistance of the crowd, pulling the lifeboat along the beach was no easy task and they had to stop several times before reaching Whitehouse Bay.

On arrival, the carriage was turned into the correct angle for launching into the surf, and my grandfather, his assistant and my father climbed into the bow of the boat. The crew had been seated from the moment they left the boathouse in order to preserve their energy for manning the oars. After the carriage had been pushed as far as possible into the surf, the coxswain gave the signal and although not quite afloat, they had been launched clear of the carriage to make full use of the oars. Launching involved the company onshore heaving on a very long length of rope through a pulley, fixed near the front wheels of the carriage to a shackle in the keel of the boat, which was then released as soon as the boat entered the water.

Within a few minutes the waves, which from the shore had not appeared to be so large, now seemed mountainous. The bow was lifted to a tremendous height, with a fair amount of water finding its way onboard. The water seemed to disappear as if by magic, but my grandfather explained that two sets of non-return valves and a special compartment ensured that the weight of the water coupled with the violent motion forced the water out through the bottom against the pressure of the sea, almost as fast as it came in.

Having pulled clear of the surf, the coxswain steered a course towards the southern end of the island, until it became obvious that the landing conditions there would be terrible and so he began a course towards the north end. Arriving there, the coxswain was able to manoeuvre the boat into such a position that they were able to scramble out onto the rocks, the parcels of food being hauled up by means of a rope.

My father's younger brother and two sisters then began running between the boat and the store carrying the parcels. They assured them that my grandmother was all right, but she had been very distressed for several hours until she recognised them in the lifeboat through the telescope. She had been under the impression that their boat had overturned at the harbour mouth, when what she saw would have been the first fishing coble that almost filled up as it crossed the bar into the harbour.

They stood outside watching until the lifeboat had been hauled up the beach at Hauxley, after which they felt that they could relax, change into dry clothing, and eat the meal that had been prepared while the lifeboat had been returning to the shore. It was usual for a few words of grace to be said, and on that day they were unanimous in offering prayers for their deliverance and for the many willing people who had assisted them. If the wind had increased in force at all, there might have been an entirely different ending. Thankfully, such an event was not repeated as the Coquet Lighthouse became equipped with a radiotelephone and large stocks of emergency provisions.

Harold Hall's painting of the lifeboat Mary Andrews heading out to Coquet Island.

Wartime at Coquet led to many unusual events, such as a torpedo mine being stranded at high tide on a northeast point of the island. My grandfather was instructed to secure it at all costs, which he did using stout manila rope. The mines were cast adrift in shipping lanes, and after sinking to a certain depth the battery driven motors would start the propeller. This would bring it to the surface at such a speed that if it hit the bottom of a ship, it would explode on impact. To the huge relief of the family, a naval party landed from a destroyer and removed the "devilish-looking" contraption. It had been bouncing about during each high water period, but luckily the rope held and kept the nose from hitting the rocks. The expert who defused it said that if it had hit the rocks, they would not have had one window left at the lighthouse!

One time when they were returning from a shopping trip at Amble, they witnessed the shelling of a merchant navy vessel by a German U-boat. It surfaced to the east of the island, and the family quickly found shelter under the lee of the rocks. Both ships were steaming at a great speed, although it was not long before the U-boat began a lively exchange of shots that lasted for about fifteen minutes. None of these shots were direct hits, but suddenly the submarine made a crash dive, presumably because another naval craft had been spotted approaching at speed. The family were hugely relieved when they were eventually able to pull around the rocks to the landing beach as some of the shells from the Merchant vessel had been a bit too close for comfort. When they looked through the telescope from the lantern gallery just after they had landed they could see her steaming towards Longstone. My father recalled the time when the Dutch liner *Queen Wilhelmina* struck a mine, and was beached just south of Hauxley. A few days after this event, the southerly winds brought wreckage of all descriptions, including furniture, rugs, medical stores and musical instruments, all of which had been spoilt by the seawater, to the landing beach at the island. Unfortunately, she could not be re-launched, and salvage work lasted several months.

One evening around 11:00 they heard a very loud explosion and all the doors in the building were flung open. Rushing outside, they could hear the drone of a Zeppelin engine and see a huge column of smoke rising from Ratcliffe colliery. To explain why the bombing had caused the doors to be flung open, my grandfather recalled that a tunnel formerly used by the Benedictine Monks to travel from the island to the mainland was aligned in the direction of this colliery. The island end of the tunnel had been bricked up when the light was established in 1839.

They could barely contain their excitement when Thomas Edwin, my father's brother, was granted a week's leave from the Seaforth Highlanders. The cruel northeast winds meant that they only glimpsed his waving figure through the telescope, however. But they were compensated when he was granted a further week's leave and the weather held good from the day he arrived until his departure.

Early in 1917 my grandfather was transferred to Flamborough lighthouse, and after that date the families at Coquet spent more time living on the mainland. Just after the end of the war the Coquet lighthouse was made a *rock station* – where families were permanently excluded.

4

Post-war lighthouse duties

It was with many regrets that my father Harold Owen Hall left Coquet early in 1917 when his father John William was transferred to Flamborough Head lighthouse. The lighthouse is situated on the cliffs at the end of the headland from the village of Flamborough, just north of Bridlington in Yorkshire.

Within a few days of arriving at Flamborough my father joined the Sea Scouts at the Naval Signal Station. He and several other scouts signed up for the Royal Navy as signallers by adding a year to their age. Signals were not difficult for my father as he had already become quite proficient in Morse and semaphore while at Coquet, where there had been a daily exchange between the signal station at Amble and the lighthouse. He was soon on duty at the naval signal station that was situated within a mile of his home, so he was often able to join his parents for a few hours at a time.

There was more wartime activity seen there than at Coquet. Guns two hundred yards away disturbed the nights by firing when Zeppelins came over, steering towards the white cliffs before turning off to raid the Humber. The signal station had communication with a gun crew about four hundred yards away on the cliff edge, by means of a field telephone. On one occasion my father was sent running to the crew with a message since the wires had been severed, and he was there long enough to see a surfaced U-Boat being fired upon. Large convoys would pass the headland and all too frequently one would be torpedoed. My father believed that over three hundred ships were sunk in the vicinity during the four years of hostilities.

1918 was a sad year for the family because they had official notification on 22ⁿᵈ March from the War Office that Thomas Edwin, my father's brother, was presumed killed in France. This was confirmed sometime afterwards.

During August of that year, my grandmother persuaded my grandfather to ask Trinity House if they would arrange my father's release. This meant that he was serving at the lighthouse as a Temporary Assistant Keeper a few weeks before the armistice was signed. The naval O.C. had wished him luck and said, "I know that your ambition is to go afloat, but you do not have much of an alternative as your mother will be much happier if you are a lightkeeper".

My father's spell of duty at Flamborough lighthouse came to an end in November 1918, and he was instructed to proceed to the Trinity House

Depot at Neyland, Pembrokeshire, for duties at Strumble Head lighthouse near Fishguard. This station was classed as a *rock light*, the families living either in Neyland or Pembroke Dock.

The senior keeper Mike Phillips knew my father very well from carrying out holiday duties at the Coquet in 1916. He sympathised with my father at the loss of his brother since he too had lost a brother. He had been drowned when his ship the Trinity House Vessel *Irene* had struck a mine in the Thames approaches.

The lighthouse at Strumble Head was actually built on an islet, known locally as Ynys Onyn. It was approached by a steel-framed bridge with a wooden planking footway. The light exhibited was a white group flasher, equipped with a triple Matthews incandescent burner and hood paraffin vapour burner. It was also fitted with an explosive fog signal that fired two shots in quick succession every ten minutes. My father remembered the details of this equipment with such clarity since he and Mike Phillips spent hours in a blizzard trying to locate and repair an electric cable that had been penetrated in several places by exploding Tonite charges.

In mid-February 1919 they returned to the Neyland Depot and towards the end of the month my father was instructed to report on board the Trinity House Vessel *Syren* for duties at the Smalls lighthouse, which lies nineteen miles off Milford Haven. As the vessel proceeded there it became obvious soon after they had cleared the Heads at the river mouth that a ground swell was beginning, enough to prevent them landing at Smalls. On the way back into the river mouth, the Captain received a message requesting him to land my father for duties at St Ann's lighthouse. It occurred to my father that the last member of the Hall family to serve there was his great grandfather John Hall during the period 1831 to 1841.

My father's spell of duty there lasted until mid July 1919, and he said he had the most wonderful time. He was free of duty every third day, which he spent fishing, swimming, or going for long walks. He was often being challenged to the fifteen-mile swim to Pembroke Dock, which he was to complete thirteen years later in only four hours and twenty minutes. Towards the end of my father's duties at St Ann's, he was left in charge for a week as his mates and all the relief keepers had contracted the Spanish influenza. The day before he left St Ann's for Whitby High Lights, he received from his father a photograph of Dale village with "Your grandfather was born in this house" written on. He remembered being annoyed with his father as he wished he had known this earlier.

When he arrived at Whitby High Lights, he was overjoyed by the welcome he received from William and Fanny Darling, his great-uncle and great-aunt. Much to their disappointment, they had been unable to have any children of their own and so they treated Harold more like a son than a great-nephew. They were delighted to be able to discuss family matters and asked him scores of questions about his grandmother, his father and mother, and of their life at Coquet Island. They were amazed to find out that the family had heard the bombardment of Scarborough, Whitby and Hartlepool by the German navy. Mr Darling had spotted them on their way north, and had been able to warn Whitby before the first shot was fired.

They enjoyed many musical evenings listening to Mr Darling on the violin accompanied by Mrs Darling on the piano, and it was always the custom to finish by singing the lightkeeper's anthem, 'Let the Lower Lights Keep Burning'. Some of the songs had been composed by William Darling, Grace's father, and handed down through three generations of the family. My father's duties at Whitby lasted from July until October 1919, when he was transferred to the Longstone lighthouse at the Farne Islands.

Having heard so much from his father about the Chathill–Seahouses railway line, he was anxious to see it for himself and to check that his father had not been joking about the rails being a different gauge to those of the mainline. When my father stepped off the Newcastle–Edinburgh mainline train at Chathill, however, he could see immediately there was a difference. His father had warned him that this train might 'dash' along at only two miles per hour, but after the engine driver had directed him to the best seat (there being no other passengers) they started off with a huge cloud of steam and he found that they were travelling at five miles per hour! Suddenly, in the middle of nowhere, he was flung violently to the floor, and poking his head out of what had at one time been a window, he saw the driver on the track looking up at him. On enquiring after the reason for the stop the driver said: "We'll let her boil up a bit", which my father found highly amusing. They had a smoke and a chat, and he declared it to have been the most enjoyable railway journey he had ever made.

Northeast gales meant that it was almost a week before he arrived at Longstone lighthouse, but this provided him with the opportunity of looking up relations and friends of the family. He had many messages of goodwill to deliver to people in the Seahouses area, some of who had attended school with his father.

Whitby High Lights, where my father completed a spell of duty in 1919. Photograph courtesy of Christopher Nicholson.

On his arrival at Longstone, my father's mates told him, "We've saved Grace's bedroom for you". Strangely enough, when my father landed there again twenty-five years later, two completely different keepers said exactly the same thing. Fixed to the wall of the room that had been Grace's was a brass plate with a description of her famous exploit. He often glanced towards the spot where the *Forfarshire* struck. In fact, just like other keepers, he always scrutinised the coastline in the dim light before dawn, hoping that he would not see what he was looking for.

When my father's spell of duty ended in the December of 1919, he was given the opportunity of seeing St Cuthbert's Chapel on Inner Farne island since the boatmen had to land some equipment there. (The light had been unmanned and working automatically for many years at that point.) St Cuthbert's original oratory, a chapel for private worship, was a very rude structure. Much later a few Benedictine monks established a small monastery, and then later the chapel was rebuilt. After Henry VIII dissolved the monasteries of England it fell into decay, and was not restored until 1848.

Another feature of great interest to him was what was left of the painting on the cliff side of a Gordon Highlander in full regalia. Although originally painted by a lightkeeper named Mackenzie, it had been repainted many times by other keepers, including his grandfather and father. It had been a talking point for hundreds of passengers on ships travelling within the inner channel for over a century.

Having been granted some leave, he returned home to Flamborough lighthouse. His father asked him so many questions about Seahouses and the islands that he would have to join his father in the lantern during the evening watch.

On 7th January 1920, he was instructed to proceed to Spurn Point Lighthouse, situated at the mouth of the Humber. The tower is 128 feet high and is built on sand dunes. This was a rather lonely land station, although there were a number of soldiers there who manned the large coastal guns. The lightkeepers could always go along to the soldier's concerts, or attend the mess canteen if they wished. My father tended to spend his off-duty periods collecting bait and setting fifty hook trotlines on the beaches. The peninsular was so narrow he was able to anchor one line on the riverside mud flat and the other on the seashore so that he was able to catch different varieties of fish.

Land light stations can also be lonely as Spurn Point proves. Photograph courtesy of Christopher Nicholson.

At this time his mother was in very poor health, so he decided to terminate his duties as a Temporary Keeper for a while. On February 12th, he arrived back home at Flamborough Lighthouse and within a very short while began work with a firm of painters and decorators. To his surprise, when knocking off for the weekend one Friday, the foreman said, "Don't bother to come in on Monday". He asked, "Do you mean I've got the sack?" and the foreman said, "No, you ass, I mean you've got a busman's holiday, because the boss has won the contract for painting your lighthouse".

5

Signing up with Trinity House

On the 23rd May 1922, my father said farewell to his family and friends and caught the train for London. To gain entry into the service of Trinity House as a Supernumerary Assistant Keeper (SAK), he had to undertake a medical examination, a written test and finally pass an oral interview with a group of committee members. My father boasted that he passed with 'flying colours'.

He was instructed to report to the superintendent at Blackwall Wharf and was then shown around by the bo'sun. He was introduced to the various departments where he would have to work at some future date in order to obtain his proficiency certificates e.g. carpenter's shop, fitters and turners and the coppersmith's. He saw the living quarters set aside for the Lights Officers, where he met some fellow SAKs.

He began a week's training at Experimental Department of Trinity House the very next day. The time flew past, since as the instructor knew that my father had previously served as a Temporary Assistant Keeper, he was simply asked to light up a few burners and was then allowed to assist the instructor with some candlepower experiments.

On May 31st, my father proceeded to the Harwich Depot to prepare for duties at the Gunfleet lighthouse, situated about seven miles off Walton-on-Naze. The red-painted Gunfleet light was built in 1850 and stood 41 feet high. The pneumatic pile method, devised in 1845 by Potts, was involved in its construction.

On arrival at the Gunfleet with one month's groceries the relief was soon carried out and he climbed from the steel platform up to the door, referred to as The Hopper by the keepers. This hinged panel of the inverted conical base had some built-in steps on the inside, hence serving the dual purpose of both door and ladder. The base was roomier than anticipated from outside due to some cleverly-designed storage. The first floor contained a small living room with a copper canopy coal range. There was also a small bedroom containing three bunks, and a small engine room that was only just large enough to house a petrol engine. This engine had only just been fitted to provide power for the radiotelephone, although the GPO cable was still in use. For example, certain pilots onboard the ships bound for the Barrow Deep Channel and the Thames would release a signal flare when passing, which the keeper on watch would reply to as well as forward to the pilot station at Harwich. On the second floor was the lantern with the paraffin vapour burner enclosed by the red shaded lens. It was the same clockwork mechanism that drove both the lens and the huge fog bell.

Gunfleet lighthouse, painted by Harold Hall in 1922.

There was very little room for exercise at that station so the keepers used to look forward to low water, especially at spring tides, as they could go for a stroll on the hard sand or play football. My father claimed that the sand was hard enough for an annual cricket match; players and spectators would arrive from Walton and Clacton in small boats.

Since the Principal Keeper knew my father well, and knew of his boating and fishing skills, he was allowed the use of the boat to add to their food stocks. It was on condition that the boat was left thoroughly scrubbed out after each fishing trip, since the boat could collect much-needed rainwater that could be used for washing. Water supply was always restricted due to lack of storage so drinking water had to be treated with value.

After four weeks duty he was instructed to return to Blackwall Wharf where he commenced training in the carpenter's, fitter's and coppersmith's shops. He was then included in the list of SAKs awaiting posts, sent when a relief keeper was required, with those whose names had been on the list longest sent first. On this occasion the list was thankfully not very long and on 7th August 1922 he was instructed to catch the Cornish Riviera from Paddington to Penzance and report to the superintendent there for duties at the Wolf Rock lighthouse.

A peculiar feature about the Wolf Rock landing is the protruding conical iron structure immediately identifying it. Formerly a marking beacon, the landing of the tower was simply constructed around it. According to my father, the Wolf Rock tower must have been one of the most difficult to construct as it was built on the pinnacle of the Wolf reef (formerly known as the Gulf reef), 17 miles from Penzance and 8 miles from the Longships tower. In terms of isolation, only Smalls lighthouse situated 19 miles off Milford Haven can compare. As well as the isolation, the east-west tidal stream forces its way through the north-south stream and the result at times has been described as a 'boiling pot', often given a wide berth by the seafarer.

Unfortunately, adverse weather conditions meant no relief could be carried out on that particular day, and the Trinity House Vessel *Mermaid* anchored in the harbour at St Mary's, Scilly Isles. My father had to find lodgings for five nights until the westerly gale that had been blowing gradually subsided. On the morning of 11th August my father re-joined the *Mermaid* on towards the Wolf Rock. Pre-landing preparations onboard the ship involved hoisting stores and gear up from the hold to be lowered into an oar-manned cutter. Landing a keeper was achieved by hauling up the man secured by what was referred to as a 'bowline on a bight'.

My father was soon enjoying a meal with his new colleagues at a dining table of a very strange design. It consisted of a circular shelf surrounding an air tube of two or three feet in diameter. The keepers would have to move their heads to speak to someone sitting at the opposite side of the pipe. He soon found out that his mandolin, for which he made a case at his Trinity House carpentry training, would be much in demand. Since in 1922 the only station boasting a gramophone was Bishop Rock, seldom an evening went by without a few requests on his mandolin. (On the one occasion when he was being landed at the Bishop Rock, one of his mates shouted, "Make his mandolin fast above the bowline, it doesn't matter if he gets wet!") His four-week period of duty passed very quickly since my father had two mates there who were highly entertaining. However, there was to be no relief at the end of the month as the storm shutters were closed and the oil lamps were lit all day. My father was introduced to Reserve Provisions, since the relief was not to arrive for another two weeks. The senior assistant keeper showed him how to place a biscuit between two pieces of clean paper, which was hammered and soaked in hot water. In 1922, the Reserve Provisions provided for keepers consisted simply of tins of corned beef, biscuits and flour.

Harold Hall on 'Bowline on a Bight' during Bishop Rock relief, New Year's day, 1923.

Although the relief was only two weeks late, the keepers were very happy when the *Mermaid* appeared on the horizon on 22ⁿᵈ September. Since so much of their limited food supply had to be thrown away, they actually had to obtain assistance from some members of the boat crew in the erection of the landing gear. The medical officer put my father on a monitored diet for some time after that, although one of his mates had to spend some time in hospital. My father attended the Penzance depot and it was decided that he could be sent to the Lizard lights for his oil engine certificate, on condition he attended the local doctor. After two visits the doctor was satisfied that my father could take on full duties again, and on 6th October he proceeded to St Anthony's lighthouse (built in 1835 with a light 72 feet above high water, situated near St Mawe's on the opposite side of the Falmouth anchorage) for special duties until the 11th October, when he was to return to Lizard and continue his training.

On 23rd October he received orders to proceed to the Bishop Rock lighthouse. Early on the morning of the 26th October the local relief boat, which was actually a small fishing trawler, chugged out of the harbour with him. It was large enough to complete the exchange of men and gear on reliefs, but heavier stores were landed at both Bishop Rock and Round Island lighthouses by the SS *Mermaid* at less frequent intervals. The Bishop Rock lighthouse was first lit in 1858 and took seven years to construct. In 1886 it was extended to its present height of 183 feet, the period of eclipse being forty-eight seconds. A double watch was maintained, one in the lantern and one in the boiler room to maintain a supply of hot air to the motors which were used to drive the revolving optic. This was the only station where this system was in use although it had been intended at the Wolf Rock light (explaining the air-pipe through the middle of the dining table mentioned previously). Other features of Bishop Rock included the hook for the mooring rope that was a permanent fixture, grouted onto the rocks with cement and boiling lead; climbing down onto the rocks to attach the mooring ropes was too risky. An additional boon was the spare room situated above the bedroom, since the number of keepers had been reduced from four to three. This room was utilised by off-duty keepers, for example playing records on the ancient gramophone or performing a few tunes on the mandolin.

My father had been looking forward to comparing the movement of the Wolf Tower with that of the Bishop Rock Tower when struck by heavy seas, for which he did not have to wait long. He found that the latter, perhaps because of its greater height, swayed more. The former tended to shake as if being struck by a hammer, although was never as bad as the Gunfleet Pile light during a north easterly gale, when it was only possible to half-fill a cup of tea during high water periods.

As the relief approached on the 23rd November the weather was calm. From Penzance he was ordered to Lizard lights for sick duties lasting about four weeks. 25th December found him once again in Penzance in order to return to the Bishop Rock. The weather was very severe and when he walked up the gangplank of SS *Peninnis* the next morning the skipper said, "I feel that I should warn you that we might have to turn back, but we are making the attempt as we are loaded with overdue goods and Christmas mail; are you a good sailor?" Having assured him that he was, they set off. He was the only passenger so enjoyed special treatment from the steward. When they reached the tidal crossroads, the Wolf tower with spray clearing the top could be seen from the port side, making a good subject for a sketch in his notebook. Over the starboard quarter there was an occasional glimpse of the Longships and Sevenstones lighthouses. All thoughts of his sketching were forgotten as he noticed that one of the ship's lifeboats had been shaken loose from its fastenings. Members of the crew were soon busy securing it. This turned out to be such a rough trip that it was late evening instead of mid-afternoon when they arrived at the harbour in St Mary's in the Isles of Scilly. While they were being tied up at the pier he noticed the huge crowd waiting for their Christmas mail.

The bad weather continued with strong westerly winds and a very heavy ground swell. Each morning my father and his mate signalled to the overdue keepers on the lighthouse to find out if all was well. An attempt was made to carry out the relief on one occasion, but conditions worsened and they had to turn back. It was not until 1st January that the 'dirty relief' occurred, all stores and gear stowed inside the tower and the entrance door closed by midday.

Although not aware of it at the time, this was to be the most exciting period of duty that my father was to experience in forty-four years of service in the lights. This was due to many occasions of extreme weather e.g. during one storm a clock was knocked off the service room wall and the mercury was shaken out of the revolving optic bath. It was commonly accepted that if the Bishop Tower could stand up to that kind of weather it could take anything.

Having volunteered to remain an extra month for a sick keeper it was early March before he set foot on firm ground, when he set off for the London Blackwall depot. Since there was a West End show that he particularly wanted to see he began to congratulate himself during the train journey, but a messenger met him at Paddington with instructions to proceed at once to Dungeness lighthouse for sick duties. He dashed over to London Bridge Station and it was not long before he was on his way. At that time, there was a railway station within a few yards of what is now referred to as the 'Old Lighthouse'. My father's disappointment at missing the show was short-lived, however, as he was to discover that he liked it very much at Dungeness.

Lizard Lights, where my father carried out sick duties in 1922. Photograph courtesy of Christopher Nicholson.

6

Further SAK training

The new lighthouse at Dungeness is a popular place with visitors, some with their fishing rods, especially since the introduction of the miniature railway from Hythe. In 1923, however, the original Dungeness lighthouse was still in use. It was 92 feet high, with a smaller tower situated 600 yards away that was built on beams to make it mobile. It was necessary to be able to adjust the lower light in order that the two lights were aligned towards the deepest part of the channel, in case of shifting shingle or sandbanks. Bideford Bar Low light, where my father had been stationed for a period, was also constructed in this way.

There was no road to the lighthouse when he arrived in early March 1923, although before he had left in June the foundations were being laid for the present road. The whole area was one vast shingle stretch, with the only footpath between the towers. 'Backstays', flat pieces of wood about one-inch thick fitted to the shoe with a leather strap, were the only way to cross the shingle. Wearing them took a lot of practice, and it was a while before my father could master the art of shuffling along as if through fresh snow.

On 20th June he travelled back to London and saw several West End shows before he received instructions to report to the Holyhead Depot for duties at Bardsey Island. On the morning of 30th June my father arrived at Holyhead Station, after catching the night train from Euston. At the Holyhead Depot he was told to board the SS *Triton* on 2nd July, thus giving him plenty of time to collect his gear and provisions for a month's duty.

The *Triton* was a small vessel of 57 tonnes, fitted with only one foremast complete with a stout derrick. By 09:00 the ship left the harbour, rounded the South Stack lighthouse, and was steaming towards the Caernarfon Bay light-vessel. There was an air of excitement onboard because it was to be the last major relief for both the *Triton* and the Caernarfon Bay light-vessel. The latter had been stationed since 1869, approximately 13 miles southwest of South Stack lighthouse, moored at a depth of over 156 feet (26 fathoms). They then landed a Blackwall mechanic at the St Tudwall Island lighthouse, before a short run to Bardsey Island, known as the Isle of a thousand Saints. Bardsey lighthouse was built in 1821 with a fog signal established in 1878, and was 99 feet high. Wives and families had lived there before it had been classed as a rock station, so was now considered to be spacious. In 1923, Bardsey was a relatively busy community compared to today; there were a number of farmers and fishermen, a small shop, a school, a chapel, and a 'King' named Christian, thus entitled due to being the oldest inhabitant, according to my father. His real name was Love Pritchard, and as he had been a sailor he would entertain my father with tales of various ports around the world. There were plenty of opportunities for exercise at Bardsey. On a clear day my father was able to climb to the top of the mountain and enjoy a rewarding view of South Stack, Holyhead Mountain, the Snowdon Range and, during a northerly wind, a glimpse of Ireland.

Trinity House depot at Holyhead.

Having completed his four-week period of duties, my father returned to Holyhead to prepare for a four-week spell at the Skerries lighthouse on the 2nd August. However, the weather was such that when they arrived at the Skerries, 7 miles off Holyhead, no relief was possible. They continued north to the Morecambe Bay lightship and then to the Selker lightship, situated off St Bee's Head near Whitehaven. The correct name for this light-vessel was the Selker

Rocks, first stationed in 1883 in sea of depth 72 feet (12 fathoms), 5 miles northwest from Selker Point. A watch buoy was moored at a fixed distance from a light-vessel in order that the master was able to frequently check his position to ensure that the light-vessel had not been dragged off its station by wind or tide, and also it provided a good guide for the watchman to check visibility when fog was approaching.

My father witnessed the roughest relief he could have imagined, and was amazed that work went on as if in the harbour instead of at sea with a gale blowing. Mooring ropes which had been trailed astern of the light-vessel were made fast to the bow of the *Triton* so the two ships were riding in line to the light-vessel's anchor cable. By means of a running line the ship's cutter was pulled backwards and forwards until the changeover of crews had been completed. When the relief was complete, the cutter was bailed out, hoisted onboard and the mooring ropes were cast off. This was followed by the usual custom of dipping the flag, signifying a courteous farewell and indicating that all was well. They then headed for the Isle of Man to investigate a complaint about the Bahama Bank buoy, before seeking shelter in Ramsey harbour.

The following day, the wind had fallen away to a calm but the visibility was rapidly falling to zero. This meant that the speed of the ship had to be reduced, especially when crossing the Liverpool Douglas route. Those who were on the after deck suddenly saw the bows of the cross-channel boat looming up a few yards from the stern. They all laughed after this close shave, but more from shaken nerves, since although the other ship slid rapidly into the fog leaving the deck awash from the wake, they only narrowly escaped collision. The fog gradually cleared away but it was late afternoon when the ship arrived at the Skerries, where landing conditions were good.

The Skerries lighthouse was established in 1714 although it was not until 1876 that a fog signal was installed. Renovations were made in 1883. The tower was 75 feet high but since it was built on a rock, the focal plane of the light was 117 feet high. My father's great grandfather John Hall had spent a great deal of his life at this station, so my father was keen to see what it must have been like. Although it was not as roomy as at Bardsey, there was plenty of opportunity for fishing. His four-week period did not seem to drag in the least and by the 3rd September he was in Holyhead again.

He was instructed to report to the depot at Neyland, Pembrokeshire, so he caught the night train and on arrival he found that he had to join the relief on the 7th September onboard the SS *Warden*. The *Warden* was 140 tonnes with seventy horsepower, was almost twice that of the Triton. He mentioned to one of the quartermasters that the *Warden* was much steadier than the *Triton* but the quartermaster said, "You wait until you see this bitch in a sea-way, she will fill up in the waist before you can move". My father found this to be true at a later date. It was not long before the ship was steaming out through the heads at St Ann's to the Skokholm Island lighthouse, five miles from St Ann's Head.

Skokholm lighthouse, where Jenny the donkey used to carry the relief gear in 1923.
Photograph courtesy of Christopher Nicholson.

The relief work at Skokholm was quite unique to him because all the gear was carried almost a mile to the lighthouse by a small gauge railway. A donkey named Jenny pulled the trucks, and was so wily that she had to be locked up in the stable the night before a relief day. This was because the ensign was only hoisted to acknowledge the approach or passing of a Trinity House vessel, and as soon as a keeper walked towards the flagstaff with the 'duster', Jenny was off with a gallop. Due to the presence of another SAK and some very good weather, my father enjoyed his four-week spell of duty at Skokholm. The keeper-in-charge remained at the lighthouse each morning while the two SAKs cleared weeds from a set amount of railway track each day.

On the morning of the 5th October, after their relief at Skokhlolm, my father then assisted with reliefs at the St Govan, Helwick, Scarweather and finally the English and Welsh grounds light-vessels. They then travelled 6 miles west to land some stores at the Flatholm lighthouse, where my father was permitted to visit. Flatholm lighthouse, a 99 feet high tower, was built on the south side of the island and first used as a beacon in 1737. It was entirely modernised in 1887 when an occulting light being was installed there. The ship steamed through the night after leaving Flatholm, heading for Lundy roads. Since it was a clear night he could identify some of the lights that he had heard so much about in his childhood, such as Bull Point where George Knott had been stationed and Hartland Point where his great uncle William Darling had served.

In the morning they set off towards the Lundy North followed by the Lundy South lighthouse, which was where he was to spend his next four weeks. The north end lighthouse tower was 56 feet in height but 165 feet above the high water mark and was built in 1897. Lundy South lighthouse was a 52 feet high tower with a focal plane 175 feet above high water mark. It was first lit in 1820 and had an explosive fog signal installed in 1878, although it was close to this station that HMS *Montague* was wrecked during dense fog in 1906. The reliefs at each lighthouse could be carried out very quickly because both stations were fitted with wire hoists – huge cables that stretched over gantries and were anchored to the nearest rocks. A motor launch was moored in position, and a hook lowered. The only difference between the two light-houses was that the gear was hoisted up to the gantry by air winches at the north end and by a steam winch at the south end. This was because the south lighthouse fired explosives during fog, and thus did not require huge reserve tanks of air to be at hand, but a donkey engine was brought into use when required to supply the steam for the north lighthouse.

a) Lundy North and b) Lundy South lighthouses, where my father was stationed in 1923.
Photographs courtesy of Christopher Nicholson.

My father recalled how the Principal Keeper at Lundy South lighthouse was a witty man from London, and also that there was quite a community of friendly people on the island. It had a small hotel, a shop and even a tiny church. A young curate there played a banjo and invited my father to bring his mandolin. The north and south lighthouses were connected by telephone, and the day after my father arrived he asked the Principal Keeper if he could call the north end to enquire about a parcel. He was told, "By all means," and was handed a pair of pliers, some spare wire and a ladder. Thankfully, my father found the break in the wire within half a mile.

The contours of the cliffs could increase the momentum of the wind during a severe gale. On one occasion during gales from the southwest, there were fifty-one ships lying behind the lee of the lighthouse and some of those on the outer fringe were rolling excessively and having to steam at anchor. This weather lasted for almost a week and one day while the keepers were enjoying a midday meal, my father recalled a large stone smashing the window and his plate. After this incident, they then fitted wire netting over all windows facing southwest.

His four-week period of duty ended all too quickly and on 6th November 1923 the SS *Warden* arrived and although the weather was rough, they had no difficulty in completing the relief due to the natural sheltered anchorage. However, on the way in to the Milford Haven River, the quartermaster's words rang true and the ship filled up to the waist. There was to be no relief at the St Govan light-vessel that day.

The keepers and lightship men were landed at the Neyland Depot the following morning and my father received instructions to proceed at once to St Catherine's Point lighthouse on the Isle of Wight. St Catherine's lighthouse, which is 84 feet high, was built in 1840. The focal plane is 134 feet due to the height of the cliff. It had a very powerful electric arc light equivalent to millions of candlepower. The engine room housed three stationary steam locomotive engines driven by coal-fired boilers with belt-driven dynamos. My father was very pleased to have the opportunity to complete his steam engine training, because both his father and grandfather had qualified in this area. During the first three weeks of his training he was required to take the first engine-room watch, just before sunset. During one of his watches a rather unusual experience occurred, which was the blowing of the packing in one of the compound cylinders. The place was full of steam within a few seconds and the only thing he could do was to start the spare engine and try to shut down the faulty one. He brought the engine to a halt by wrapping a piece of wire around a pole, and then advised the engineer in charge through the speaking tube. Tragically, three keepers lost their lives in that engine room during the Second World War due to a low flying raider.

It was with some regret that my father left the Isle of Wight on 29th December 1923, but soon found himself in London again. He called the Blackwall Depot, and found that he had been granted leave. He was on the first northbound train the next day, arriving at Flamborough Lighthouse in the evening much to the surprise of everyone. The lighthouse there was built in 1806, the actual height to the lantern gallery being 87 feet. In 1878, a gun station was established two hundred yards to the east on the cliff edge, conducting experiments in how the sound of a fired rocket compared to a signal muzzle-loading gun. As a result, the rocket replaced the signal gun at Lundy, Smalls, Heligoland and Tusker Rock lighthouses, although it was not until the turn of the century that a siren was installed at Flamborough lighthouse.

He carried out sick duties at Flamborough lighthouse from 6th until 29th January 1924, until he was posted at Souter Point lighthouse, situated in the village of Marsden between the River Tyne and Sunderland. The tower was built in 1871 and was 76 feet high with a focal plane 150 feet above the high water mark. A foghorn was established in the same year.

Souter Point lighthouse, built in 1871. Photograph courtesy of Christopher Nicholson.

He received a telegram on 10th February, and knew the contents before opening it. My father's mother was dying, and it was not long before he requested leave to attend her funeral in Flamborough. The family were touched by the large attendance. His parents were held in very high esteem by local people, as were his grandparents by the older inhabitants. They had attended the funeral of Thomas Owen Hall who had been the principal keeper at that station for many years, and died on duty in 1899. His father John William Hall was moved when the assistant keepers lowered the ensign at the lighthouse and the signal stations during the funeral procession.

John William Hall, my grandfather, aged 58 years.

After his mother had died in 1924, his father was transferred to Bull Point light in North Devon. His next and last transfer was to Penlee fog station, a familiar sight to seafarers sailing in and out of Plymouth. In 1934 my grandfather John William Hall retired from the service and lived in Plymouth until he died in 1957, having completed forty-five years in the service of Trinity House, forty-two of which had been as a lightkeeper. My grandmother had served as an official assistant keeper for two years.

Having returned to London at the end of the month my father found that on the 5th March he was travelling north to Whitby High Lights to carry out sick duties followed by holiday duties. During his off-duty hours he was able to walk the three-mile distance to Whitby to visit Mr and Mrs Darling, who had retired there in 1919. His duties ended on 7th June when he proceeded to Flamborough lighthouse until 21st July and then Souter Point lighthouse until 15th August, when he began six weeks holiday duties at St Mary's island lighthouse, situated between the river Tyne and Blythe harbour. This lighthouse is a white painted tower 120 feet high. It was built in 1898 on the site of what was formerly known as St Mary's Chapel. Apart from the wreck of the SS *California* on 15th January 1913, there were very few casualties whereas previous to 1898 there were many, for example, the *Longhurst* in 1878, the *City of Gothenburg* in 1891 and the SS *Springer* in 1892.

In September he returned to Blackwall Depot in London before proceeding to Bull Point lighthouse, situated near Ilfracombe in North Devon. He did not mention that his father was stationed at Bull Point, but packed up in record time and could only relax once the train had left Paddington Station. Since he was worried that the assistant keepers would accuse the son of the principal of receiving preferential treatment, he thought he had better keep it to himself. Things could not have been farther from the truth, however, since although my father received excellent reports from other principal keepers, he only managed to scrape a "fairly good" from John William. During their family reunion, he not only enjoyed working with his father but also spending off-duty time with his brother and sisters.

Unfortunately, he was transferred once more to Bideford Bar lights on 3rd November 1924, situated at the mouth of the Bideford River amongst the sand dunes. Winter duties lasted four months, ensuring three keepers for the longer nights as opposed to two during the summer. The tower there exhibited a white light, with a 30-second period of eclipse, at a height of 93 feet above the high water mark. It was built in 1820 of wood and finished off with solid oak tiles. A smaller light was exhibited aligned with the entrance of the river, which was changed from white to red according to the level of the tide. 'Blinking Billy', an automatic light situated some distance along the shore, did not require much attention beyond filling it with lythene. The method of operation was very ingenious, as it consisted of a small flame jet that generated enough heat to revolve a shutter around it. The minor drawback, however, was that the speed at which the shutter revolved was dependent upon outside temperature. Many keepers and their families found Bideford a very isolated station. My father remembered that great care had to be taken with food to ensure that fine sand did not penetrate after a gale of wind.

Harold Owen (left) with his brother John William and their father, John William Hall.

He escaped from Bideford during February as he was ordered to Hartland Point for sick duties, but had to return on 3ʳᵈ March. Hartland tower, built in 1874, was only 59 feet high with a focal plane at a height of 120 feet. After winter duties he was posted at Lynmouth Foreland lighthouse, 55 feet high, although 400 feet above the high water mark as it was perched on the side of a cliff from which stones would rattle down into the courtyard. The tower was built at a lower level than the dwellings, so a keeper would say that he was "going down to light up". His holiday duties continued throughout the summer of 1925 at Bull Point, Bideford Bar and Hartland Point. On 12th October he was ordered to Burnham lighthouse, situated near Weston-super-Mare. The principal keeper and his wife could not take their holiday together since one of them had to remain at the station. Burnham lighthouse, 99 feet high, was built in 1832 at a distance of approximately 1,000 feet from the shoreline. A smaller tower, thirty-six feet high, was built on piles close to the high water mark in 1897. The high light was visible for up to fifteen miles, but the low light was only visible for nine.

The low light at Burnham, built on piles next to the high water mark. Photograph courtesy of Christopher Nicholson.

On 24th November he returned to the Blackwall depot and was on his way to the Gunfleet lighthouse two weeks later. On 7th December 1925 he joined the SS *Satellite* that steamed out on what was referred to as the north relief. He was on board as it was possible that there could have been time to land him at the Gunfleet that night, but it turned out that he was not landed there until the 12th December. On the north relief, the ship steamed out past the Cork light-vessel (an experimental automatic ship) off Felixstowe, to complete a relief at the Shipwash light-vessel off Southwold. From the Shipwash the ship steamed in an easterly direction towards the Outer Gabbard light-vessel and then the Galloper light-vessel. The Galloper was first established as far back as 1803, the Shipwash in 1837, the Cork in 1840, and the Outer Gabbard in 1888.

On the south relief, the first port of call was the Sunk light-vessel established in 1802. Following this, they called at the Longsand light-vessel situated seven miles southeast of the Sunk, first stationed in 1883, and then at the Kentish Knock light-vessel nine miles from the Longsand and two miles northeast of the Middle Knock buoy. From there, the ship proceeded to the Edinburgh Channel light-vessel and anchored for the night. After calling at the Barrow Deep light-vessel the following day, he and the other reliefs were landed at the Gunfleet.

On the morning of 31st March 1926, after a short period in London waiting for his name to reach the top of the list of SAKs, my father received urgent orders to relieve a sick man at the Gunfleet Lighthouse. This became the speediest journey that he ever made to a rock station from the Blackwall Depot. When he arrived at 19:00 that evening, his mates at the Gunfleet could not believe that he had only left the Depot at 11:00 that morning. His speed was due to a combination of a lift from a kind-hearted lorry driver, an sympathetic bus driver and the fact that the west-bound train was just on the point of steaming out of the Bromley-by-Bow Metropolitan station when he arrived there. He had returned to London by 11th April, on 3rd May he travelled on the Cornish Riviera to Penzance *en route* to the Bishop Rock. The next day he went to the Isles of Scilly on the SS *Scillonian*, a new ship that was owned by the inhabitants of the islands. After three days in Hughtown he was landed at the Bishop Rock for duty until the 5th June. On the 6th June after one night ashore he was landed at Round Island lighthouse for one month's duty. Round island is one of the most northerly of the group of islands, and the lighthouse, sixty three feet in height, was built in 1887 with a focal plane of 180 feet above high water mark.

Round Island lighthouse, situated on one of the most northerly of the Isles of Scilly. Photograph courtesy of Christopher Nicholson.

Following his Round Island duty, he returned to London and, in view of the number of SAKs waiting at Blackwall, it seemed a good time to request leave. However, on the 26th August he travelled to Spurn Point lighthouse, via Hull and Partington. The final seven miles of the journey were made in a trap pulled by a pony over sand dunes. Spurn Point lighthouse, 128 feet in height and built in 1776, was painted black with a white band around it. He had been stationed there before when serving as a temporary assistant keeper, and so was quite familiar with the layout of the place. He soon became acquainted with many new members of the community, including coast guards, boatmen and some of the troops who manned the coastal guns.

On 9th September he was transferred to Withernsea lighthouse, 127 feet high and built in 1891, which was a white painted tower. On 5th November he was on his way to Holyhead to join the Skerries lighthouse for four weeks quarterly duties, after which he was sent to Bardsey Island. Unfortunately, he had to be brought ashore on the 26th December to Aberdaron for medical attention. He was extremely grateful to the islanders who brought him across during some strong tides as well as to the family who kept the hotel at Aberdaron and the doctor who removed some particles of steel from one of his eyes. On 28th January 1927 he was declared fit for work and was on his way to Holyhead for duties at the Breakwater lighthouse. It had been built in 1872 at the end of Holyhead breakwater and exhibited a red flashing light known as a fixed flasher. The beehive-top prisms were arranged to throw a continuous beam of light a distance of three to four miles, for the benefit of inshore craft.

His duties at Breakwater were completed on 4th April and he travelled by taxi to South Stack lighthouse, a few miles from Holyhead. South Stack tower is 91 feet high, had been in operation since 1809 and had a new fog horn installed in 1895. The keepers also had to operate the submarine bell for the cross channel boats to Ireland, although this equipment was phased out.

On 9th May the Trinity House vessel beacon arrived and my father was able to land within a few hours from her at the Skerries lighthouse for another four-week period of duty. However, on 7th June he was brought ashore and given urgent instructions to catch the first train from Holyhead to Penzance for sick duties at Longships lighthouse. On arrival at Penzance he was ordered to Sennen Cove, situated near Lands End, but due to bad weather it was not until the 10th June that he was landed at the Longships. The Longships Tower was built of granite, 117 feet high and first lit in 1795, with an explosive fog signal established later in 1898. He claimed that it was more comfortable in heavy weather at Longships than either Wolf or Bishop Rock since a ledge close to the base of the tower reduced the momentum of the waves.

Withernsea lighthouse, where my father was posted for two months in 1926.
Photograph courtesy of Christopher Nicholson.

The granite tower of Longships, first lit in 1795. Photograph courtesy of Christopher Nicholson.

Pendeen Point lighthouse, where my father completed a spell of duty in 1927. Photograph courtesy of Christopher Nicholson.

After four weeks duty at the Longships he came ashore and carried out nine weeks holiday duties at Pendeen Point lighthouse, situated near the village of that name close to Cape Cornwall and the Lavant Tin Mine. During his off-duty periods he was able to visit some of his relatives in St.Ives, Helston and Truro on his motorcycle. After the holiday duties, he was granted some leave of his own that he spent at Penlee Fog Station near Plymouth where his father was posted, after which he returned to Blackwall leaving his motorcycle at home.

Winter duties, lasting over five months, were spent at Souter Point lighthouse from 30th September 1927 until early March 1928. He was then ordered to Flamborough Head lighthouse for sick duties and as this had previously been his home, he saw a number of friends before returning to Blackwall at the end of the month.

After two days in London he caught the train for Plymouth for duties at the Eddystone lighthouse for a four-week period after which he was posted to the North Foreland lighthouse. The lighthouse there was established as a Beacon in 1636, but changes in illumination took place in 1880 and 1891 and navigational aids have been added in order to keep in step with progress. The white painted tower is 85 feet in height, with a focal plane of 188 feet above the high water mark.

He returned to London on 31st May to find that he was the only available SAK. Within a few hours he was bound for Weymouth to catch the night boat to Guernsey, which he remembered as a very rough trip. He was landed on 2nd June 1928 at Casquets lighthouse, nine miles from Alderney. Casquets was first established as a beacon in 1723 and restored in 1891.

On 18th July he left Paddington for Haverfordwest in Pembrokeshire for sick duties at St Ann's lighthouse near Milford Haven and on the last day of the month he returned again to Blackwall.

On 21st August 1928 he caught the river steamer from the Woolwich pier to Margate for duties at North Foreland lighthouse, although normally he would have travelled by rail. However, the previous evening, he had bought a box of sweets at the cinema while on a date. The box of sweets contained a 'lucky number', which won him the river steamer ticket. The following day, he was astonished when he telephoned for orders and was told to travel to North Foreland for sick duties!

On his return to London from North Foreland there were so many SAKs waiting for instructions that many, including himself, were granted leave. He said he was on the first train to Plymouth, *en route* to Penlee Point.

In November he and another SAK were detailed for radio beacon instructions at Round Island lighthouse and although the journey to Penzance and the Isles of Scilly was no novelty to either of them, they both agreed that it was a pleasant change to be travelling in company. By the time they returned to London again the year 1928 had almost come to an end and my father was promoted to Assistant Keeper to the South Bishop lighthouse, situated near St David's Head in Pembrokeshire.

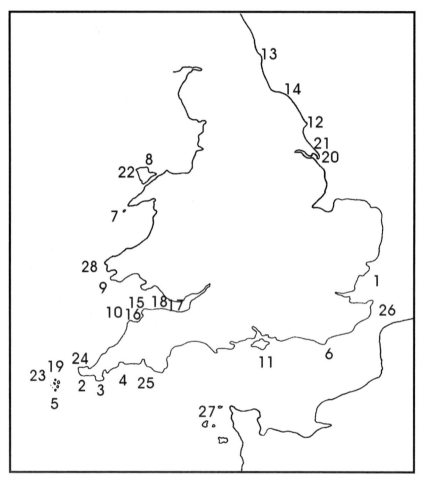

1. Gunfleet	11. St Catherine's	21. Withernsea
2. Wolf Rock	12. Flamborough	22. Holyhead Breakwater
3. Lizard Lights	13. Souter Point	23. Longships
4. St Anthony's	14. Whitby High Lights	24. Pendeen Point
5. Bishop Rock	15. Bull Point	25. Eddystone
6. Dungeness	16. Bideford Bar Lights	26. North Foreland
7. Bardsey Island	17. Lynmouth Foreland	27. Casquets
8. Skerries	18. Burnham	28. St Ann's Head
9. Skokholm	19. Round Island	
10. Lundy South	20. Spurn Point	

The 28 lighthouses where Harold Hall worked as SAK from May 1922 until the end of 1928, when he was promoted to the post of Assistant Keeper.

7

Promotion, a wife and a daughter: South Bishop and Orfordness

In 1929, the keepers at South Bishop, Smalls and Skokhom lighthouses lived in Pembroke Dock during their periods of shore leave. They worked at the rock lighthouses (i.e. without families) for eight weeks followed by a four-week period of leave. My father settled into this rota very quickly after arriving at the South Bishop lighthouse in February. After six years of carrying everything with him from place to place, it was wonderful to have his own room in which to leave his personal belongings. During clear weather, the Irish coast could be seen quite clearly. Skokholm lighthouse lay five miles southwest and Smalls lighthouse twelve miles due west.

The South Bishop Tower, built in 1839, was only 36 feet in height, although it stood 144 feet above the high water mark. In 1883, the procedure during fog was to fire two rockets every fifteen minutes. At the time of his service, the signal was a siren that sounded four blasts at intervals. In this way it was similar to Whitby High lights, referred to as 'The Whitby Cow' by the locals. He recalled one occasion during heavy fog when the fog signal broke down at the South Bishop, even though replacements were held for most of the equipment. My father had been asked by the senior keeper to climb down the rocks and try to contact a ship using Morse code. Taking a powerful torch, he managed to contact a tugboat that passed the message to Trinity House, Swansea. Luckily, engineers were able to repair the fault within hours. They were extremely grateful when they could sound the fog signal again, as they had been very uneasy during the forty-eight-hour breakdown.

The general layout at South Bishop was similar to North Lundy light-house, in that it was also fitted with a wire hoist driven by an air winch. This made very short work of hoisting half a dozen relief boxes from the boat to the Gantry platform, or even a couple of 40 gallon drums of oil. My father recalled how there were sixteen workmen carrying out renovations, including building an annexe to the engine room for the new radiotelephone and radio beacon, as well as a new winch room and gantry platform for the wire hoist. The blacksmith working there complained because the highly tempered cutting tools had to be re-sharpened after just a few strikes of the hammer on the rock. The workmen were not always grumpy, however, since on many occasions he had sixteen workmen enthusiastically singing along to his mandolin.

South Bishop Tower, my father's first post as Assistant Keeper in 1929. Photograph courtesy of Christopher Nicholson.

During his shore leave periods he got around in his bull-nosed Morris to places such as Manobier, Bosheston Lakes or Solva and he sketched the South Bishop from Whitesand Bay near St David's Head. But my father didn't just sketch when onshore; he also found time for courting. He married my mother Josephine on 14th February 1932 in Llanstadwell Church in Neyland. Apparently, he asked the Vicar if he and my mother could have a quiet wedding, although he detected a hint of a smile when the Vicar replied, "We will try". He recalled how as he was being lowered in the bowline from the lighthouse his mates were shouting, "Good luck!" while showering him and the boat crew with rice. Since the wedding was held a few minutes after the Sunday morning service, where my mother had been a popular chorister, everyone stayed to witness the wedding and enjoy the choral service. Evidently there was a large crowd waiting at the church long before the wedding ceremony took place. It was reported in the local press how "The bride, who presented a charming picture, was attired in an ankle-length dress of ivory satin, with veil and orange blossom and shoes to tone". My mother carried a bouquet of white heather carnations, lilacs and fern. Her bridesmaids were her sister May and Ivy Trott from Pembroke Dock, who wore blue ankle-length dresses made of satin. A reception was held at my mother's family's home before the proud Mr and Mrs Hall left by car for their new home in Pembroke Dock.

The wedding of my parents, Harold and Josephine.

Three years later, in February 1935, my father was transferred to
Orfordness lighthouse in Suffolk, which was at that time a two-handed
land station with dwellings attached. Orfordness tower, which my parents
enjoyed very much, was built in 1792 and renovated in 1888. It is 99 feet in
height and painted red with white bands. As it was surrounded by shingle, it
reminded my father of Dungeness lighthouse. They had to cross the River
Ore by boat, which took only a few minutes, before they could go shopping
in Orford village.

Orfordness lighthouse with my father in the foreground,
where my parents moved in 1935.

Coast guards and lightkeepers saw quite a lot of each other as the lookout hut was only fifty yards from the lighthouse and the keepers often strolled over for a chat. My father remembered two occasions when he didn't stroll, but ran over. The first occasion was when he saw a rocket being fired a few miles to the north and after a certain amount of hesitation, he got the guard on duty to telephone the coast guard nearest to the estimated location of the rocket. They later discovered that there had been a fireworks display at a school. The headmaster was alarmed to discover how far down the coast the rocket had been seen. On the second occasion, there was no hesitation. One of my father's hobbies at the time was constructing small radio receivers and he was trying out a new coil when he started to write down a message, realising it was an SOS in Morse code. My father ran over to the coast guard and within minutes they had worked out the given position and had informed the lifeboat crew.

Orfordness lighthouse was designated as a rock station in 1937, and so my parents had to find accommodation in Dovercourt, Essex. It was here that I was born on 27th August 1937 although not baptised until a later date in St Augustine's Church where my father and his brother had been choristers. My father said that the ceremony was very nostalgic for him. Not long after I was born my parents moved into a larger house and my father joined my mother every third month when on shore leave. After about 18 months my father received his transfer papers from Trinity House: he was instructed to move to St Mary's Lighthouse near Whitley Bay in Northumberland.

8

The Second World War: St Mary's Island

I was 18 months old when my parents moved to St Mary's lighthouse in February 1939. St Mary's is a land station, meaning that families could live on the lighthouse with the keepers. Many years ago St Mary's Island was called Bate Island after it's owner, Thomas Bates, who was a surveyor for the north for Queen Elizabeth I. During medieval times, there was a chapel dedicated to St Helen that had an endowment of five shillings a week. There were many such coastal chapels displaying lights to help mariners, referred to as 'Our Lady's Lights', or 'St Mary's Lights'. At one time there was a graveyard on St Mary's Island for shipwrecked mariners. When the lighthouse was built in 1897 the mariners' remains were exhumed and reburied at Seaton Delaval nearby. St Mary's also has an old stone house, built in 1855, which apparently was an alehouse.

St Mary's lighthouse, painted by my father Harold Hall in 1966.

St Mary's Island, an island at high tide only, is situated between Whitley Bay and Blythe in Northumberland. At low tide it is linked to the mainland by a causeway. When we lived at St Mary's there were large stepping-stones alongside the causeway, for when it had just been covered by the tide. These stepping-stones weren't completely safe, however, as the public would turn over the stones to search for winkles. One day my father stood on a loose stepping-stone while carrying me across to the mainland on his back. Before I knew it, I was on my back in the water feeling rather startled, wet and cold, my best blue coat keeping me afloat.

Eight months after we arrived at St Mary's the Second World War broke out. Several representatives from the armed forces came to persuade my mother to evacuate the lighthouse, but even the thought of being cut off from the mainland in the event of an invasion did not deter her. Although my father was concerned for our safety he respected her wishes and so it was finally settled – we were to be at St Mary's for the duration of the war.

There was an army camp and rifle range on the coastline opposite the lighthouse. The soldiers aimed at targets situated in front of two large mounds of earth called butts. As we had to walk along the road between the back of the butts and the cliff edge on our way to the main Whitley Bay road, trips to town were limited. One day when my mother and I were on our way back from town, we stopped at the sentry box and explained our intention to go back to the lighthouse. The sentry picked up the receiver of the field telephone, turned the handle around as fast as he could, and spoke into the mouthpiece. He received clearance and we could see the warden bringing down the red flag and so set off along the road between the back of the butts and the cliff edge. But while we were still behind the butts, someone opened fire! As mother and I made an urgent dash to the safety of the pits, the firing stopped as suddenly as it had begun.

The soldiers also had to learn how to throw hand grenades, and they used to throw them from the cliffs opposite the lighthouse. In addition to this, a target plane would often fly overhead and an anti-aircraft gun would open fire at the target being pulled along at safe distance behind the aircraft. When I saw the planes in the distance I used to rush indoors as I found the noise unbearable.

Due to a combination of the military activity and the tides it was inadvisable for me to start school at the age of five, so my mother approached the education authorities and told them of our plight. They provided my mother with advice and books for her to teach me herself for the first year of my educational life. One of the first things she taught me was how to write my own name. When I mastered this I wrote my name all over our neighbour's wooden fence. I was rather pleased with my achievement and was surprised when our neighbour stopped me a few days later and told me not to do it again as it made the fence look unsightly. I ran in to tell my mother what had happened, and remember asking, "How did he know it was me?"

A photograph of my parents and me, taken in 1940

When I finally went to school in Whitley Bay there were many difficulties to overcome. Being an island at high tide meant that I could only attend school for part of the day, the particular part being different each week. Although the other children initially thought I was lucky to avoid so much school, it made my progress very difficult and then led them to make unkind remarks.

The tides were not my only enemy when trying to get to school, as I also had to contend with the firing range. My parents would telephone the warden to say that we were leaving the lighthouse, and he would stop the firing. For the first six months of attending school, when my mother accompanied me on my journey to Whitley Bay, everything ran smoothly, but the time came when I had to make the journey on my own. My mother contacted the warden as usual and I set off from the lighthouse with my satchel on my back and my gas mask. I crossed the causeway without a hitch, and walked towards the first sentry. He shouted, "Halt! Who goes there?" When I replied, "Pat, the girl from the lighthouse", he looked at me suspiciously. He asked me my destination, but seemed unwilling to believe me. I remember feeling trapped between the sharp end of his bayonet and the edge of the cliff. Finally, he telephoned the warden who confirmed my identity and business.

At the end of my school day I would walk to the station to catch the bus home. I remember being panicked when the bus conductress shouted, "Workers only" and would not allow me to board the bus. This also distressed my mother because not only did I arrive home late, but had risked missing the tide and being stranded on the mainland.

I made a few friends at school and they invited me to their birthday parties. As it was difficult to buy toys during wartime my father made toys for me to take as presents. He made a doll's cot and doll's house for me. I had great fun with the doll's house, especially closing the imitation 'black-outs' at night. Doll's house furniture was difficult to find. One Christmas my mother's sister made me a dressing table out of matchboxes, shoe buttons for knobs and a makeup handbag mirror. My father made a swing for me to play with, on which I spent hours imagining I was flying in an aeroplane. It was not possible to buy sophisticated dolls as all money and materials were diverted to the war-effort, although my mother tried unsuccessfully to win me a doll in a charity raffle. When it was too wet or blustery to play outside I retreated to a room where the oil lamps were stored, oblivious to my mother creeping around outside.

While living at St Mary's, we had a beautiful black cat called Smut. Smut's favourite pastime was catching rats over on the mainland. He usually came back before the tide covered the causeway but on one occasion my father, watching from the lantern room at the top of the lighthouse, saw Smut jumping across the stepping-stones. If the distance was too great for him to jump, he swam instead of being trapped on the mainland. I'm sure the lighthouse gave Smut the same feeling of security that it gave me. I loved sitting in our snug kitchen on winter evenings when the cold wind whistled around the house, and the waves were beating against the rocks.

Food was in short supply during the war and everything was subject to rationing. People were encouraged to be resourceful. Mr Crisp, our neighbour, kindly lent my father his rowing boat to go fishing. My father used to put down lobster pots and we also took our fishing lines out. My parents also used to grow vegetables in the garden such as potatoes, cabbage, and lettuce. However, such things as eggs, butter and fruit were scarce. Every time I was spreading butter on my bread my mother would urge me to scrape it on. In the absence of fresh eggs, my mother used powdered egg. She was occasionally allowed a couple of bananas as she had a child. Although my mother didn't consider sweets were all that good for me, she would allow me a few as an occasional treat, such as some unwrapped boiled sweets. My mother used to make up for the lack of vitamins by making me take cod liver oil and malt extract. The malt extract suited my sweet tooth, but I only tolerated the cod liver oil to keep her happy.

As it was impossible for the milkman, postman or paperboy to make deliveries to our doorstep, some boxes were erected on the mainland large enough to hold our milk, mail and papers. When the tide permitted, the keepers took it in turns to walk over the causeway and collect the deliveries. My mother used to order her groceries from a shop in Whitley Bay for delivery by the van driver. Deliverymen were the only people, apart from the lighthouse keepers and their families, who were permitted to pass the sentry. When the groceries kept failing to arrive, however, my mother called the shop to complain. She found out that the sentries were refusing him access as there was another van delivering groceries to the lighthouse. My parents had seen this other van, and suspected that it was unauthorized. The military were informed, the mysterious van disappeared, and the grocery van was allowed to deliver our food again.

There was a shortage of books during wartime. My mother would cut out the Rupert Bear daily instalments from my father's newspaper and stick them in an exercise book so that I could look at them whenever I wanted. People didn't throw anything away that could be recycled. I remember a neighbour giving me a nursery rhyme book that had pages held together with sticky plasters.

My mother and father occasionally took me to a pantomime or the cinema in Newcastle-upon-Tyne. I remember returning from Newcastle-upon-Tyne on the bus, after a visit to the theatre. It seemed very eerie sitting on the top deck of the bus in the darkness, as no lights were allowed. The headlights were only strong enough for the driver to see where he was going. When we finally reached our bus stop we had to use a torch covered with paper to dim the light. My mother and father always advised me to keep the beam down, and not to point the torch up at the sky. On winter evenings it seemed an endless walk down the road with the icy wind biting into us, and it was a relief to arrive home.

My mother had several favourite filmstars, but Charles Boyer topped the bill. On one occasion in 1941, when everyone was talking about a possible enemy invasion, my mother went to the cinema on her own to see a Charles Boyer film. By the time she left the cinema, caught the bus from the centre of Whitley Bay to the cemetery, and began the walk down the road towards the cliff, dusk was setting in. Her head was still full of thoughts of invasion. Suddenly, in the half-light, she could see men with helmets on, carrying rifles, running up over the cliff. "It's the invasion!" she told herself. She didn't know whether it was best to walk calmly towards them, or to turn around and run back towards the cemetery. She decided to keep walking towards the soldiers and was relieved when she heard a voice saying, "Good evening, Ma'am". Charles Boyer or not, my mother decided it might be best to avoid the cinema for a while, at least until her imagination calmed down.

At the beginning of the war the Government decided that in case of a gas attack the public were to be issued with masks. My parents received theirs first and they encouraged me to put their gas masks on so that I could become accustomed to it. I was therefore not afraid when I collected my own mask, which for young children had Mickey Mouse printed on it. I had to queue up with other children to be fitted, some of who were protesting loudly. The organisers wanted me to stay to demonstrate to other children how harmless the masks were, but my mother said we had to return to the lighthouse before the tide came over the causeway.

When the air raids began, it was hard for my mother to take them seriously. She did not like leaving her warm bed in the middle of the night to find her way down to the cold shelter. One night after the air raid sirens had stopped, I felt rather frightened and crept in beside my mother. She was also feeling a little nervous and decided that we should seek refuge under the kitchen table for a while. Suddenly, we heard a loud bang and the sound of breaking glass. A land mine had been dropped and had exploded near the cemetery at the top of the road. The blast blew our bedroom windows out! My father rushed in from the lighthouse tower to see if we were all right. When we finally went upstairs to investigate, we found the glass strewn across the bedroom where my mother had been sleeping. After that incident, we always went down to the basement during air raids. We were always warned of imminent raids by a siren at Whitley Bay. When I heard the siren, I would stand up in my cot, grab my teddy bear, and shout at the top of my voice. I thought that if I shouted loud enough, I could block out the sound of the anti-aircraft gun at the army camp. Soldiers would begin to fire their guns minutes after the siren ceased. My mother would run into my room, grab me in her arms still screaming, and rush down two flights of stairs into the basement – all in semi-darkness. We would sit in the basement for what would seem like hours, listening to the explosions outside, until the 'all clear' siren could be heard.

Fortunately, there weren't any air raids during school although we did have air raid practice. When a bell went we had to rush out into the playground and be ready to run into the shelters. There were frequent raids on the northeast coast during the early days of the war, however. On one occasion my father told me how a raider dropped a bomb on the rocks near our house when the door was open, and the blast was so fierce that its effect was felt on the upper floor where the long curtains above my cot had become twisted. Although I wasn't aware of it at the time, it was very unsafe to be in the lighthouse courtyard during an air raid, due to the cone of fire erected by the Tyne barrage.

It was not uncommon to come across small bombs that had been washed up by the tide. They were very colourful – yellow and green – and had handles making them very tempting to pick up. However, I had received repeated warnings from my mother and father not to touch them as they were deadly weapons, and so I managed to restrain myself. On one or two occasions we saw mines floating past the lighthouse wall at high tide. One day my mother and I were walking around the island to get some fresh air, and suddenly noticed that we were within two or three yards of a large mine that had been washed up at high tide. We immediately turned around and ran for the safety of the lighthouse. Ships passing St Mary's lighthouse were sometimes blown up when colliding with mines. My father said that on more than one occasion he had grabbed the telephone to summon the lifeboat to a mined ship even before "the gusher of spray" had time to disappear. He recalled the occasion when the *Pandora*, about five thousand tonnes, struck twin mines northeast of St Mary's while on tow from the Tyne to Blyth. Another time, a smaller vessel named the *Mars* struck a mine between St Mary's lighthouse and the Tyne, taking about ten minutes to sink due to her cargo of timber. The Tyne pilot cutter assisted by the Blythe lifeboat arrived quickly to pick up the crew. When my father described the sinking of an ammunition ship during an air raid, he said the blast was so severe that a piece of derrick had been found in the Rothbury Hills, 12 miles away.

My father reminded me of the time one of our own aircraft, a Hampden bomber, was in trouble. Although it had a deadly cargo, it circled the light-house for some time to use up fuel as one of its engines had failed. This was the first occasion that my father received an SOS message in Morse from an aircraft, but there was little anyone could do apart from search the rocks after the accident. The keepers heard that some of the crew had jumped from the aircraft inland, but unhappily there were no survivors. The pilot had tried to land in a field without the bombs exploding, but was unsuccessful.

I remember when my father wanted to take a photograph of me standing on the causeway with the lighthouse in the background. I saw an aeroplane and pointed to it, and my father looked up and realised it was a German reconnaissance aircraft. Needless to say, we made a quick dash for the lighthouse.

On another occasion, the Royal Navy visited us unexpectedly. A submarine was being towed by a ship and ran onto the rocks during thick fog. My father was on the rocks with a loud hailer trying desperately to warn them of the danger. He let the commander of the submarine come ashore to use the telephone at the lighthouse, afterwards accompanying the commander back to the submarine. The Blyth lifeboat took the crew off first, leaving the senior officers on board until the submarine and the ship were finally pulled clear on the rising tide.

People were not encouraged to travel during wartime unless their journey was really necessary. However, my mother felt she had to get away from St Mary's Island once a year to visit relatives. My grandfather Hall lived with my Aunt and Uncle in Plymouth, and my maternal grandmother lived in South Wales, where she had lived ever since my mother was 12 years old. She lived in a bungalow full of interesting paraphernalia. Her son, who was a seafaring man like his father before him, used to bring back trinkets from all over the world. I would spend hours looking at all the exquisite items.

I recall that there were no lights on trains and the station platforms were full of servicemen. On one occasion when travelling to Plymouth, the air-raid siren began just as we arrived at Kings Cross Station. We ran towards the nearest underground station, and were asked directions by an American Serviceman. I remember that once we had reached the safety of the shelter, he offered me some 'candy' and 'chewing gum'.

Visiting Plymouth was always disheartening as it was bombed heavily. Every time we visited the city there seemed to be yet another pile of rubble and bomb damage where a shop or house had once stood. My Uncle Dan, who was a policeman, received the British Empire Medal from the King and Queen at Buckingham Palace for rescuing several people from a burning house. It was encouraging when, after the war, one could see Plymouth rise from the dust and become a thriving city once more. Despite the bomb damage, my aunt, uncle and grandfather were cheerful people and always had an interesting tale to tell.

On the day that peace was declared, my mother cried. I suppose it was the strain of the preceding years. When she had gathered her senses together, she said, "Let's celebrate with a cup of tea!"

9

Peacetime and a transfer

Now that the war was over, visitors were once more allowed to come to St Mary's Island. The café and the lighthouse re-opened their doors to the public, and an air of normality began to settle over St Mary's. Evelyn Laye, popular in musicals, visited St Mary's while taking time out from a show in Newcastle-upon-Tyne. I was fascinated by her red-painted toenails, and remember bending down for a closer look. My mother was horrified, but Miss Laye kindly let me touch them.

Visitors found it hard to believe that there were families living on the island. Sometimes my mother would let me paddle my feet in a rock-pool as she watched from a safe distance, and it was never long before the visitors would surround me, saying things like, "Look at this poor child, I wonder where she comes from", while offering me sweets or money. They were always relieved when my mother came rushing up and they realised I hadn't been abandoned.

One time when I was at school, two elderly ladies visited and my father told them of his daughter Pat who wanted a doll that could open and close its eyes. When they asked where I was, he told them they might meet me on my way home from school. I did meet them, and they explained to me that they had been talking to my father in the lighthouse, and we chatted for a while about all kinds of things. After waving goodbye I didn't expect to hear from them again, but several weeks later my mother received a letter from one of the ladies. She said she had tried all the shops in London she could think of, without success, and that she had been in touch with her relations in Canada to ask them to buy a doll and send it to St Mary's lighthouse. Finally, a rather battered cardboard box arrived from Canada. My mother took it upstairs to open, as she was rather worried about the condition of the contents. It was the doll, and, apart from a broken finger and eyelid, in good working order. I called her Rosalie. We made a lasting friendship with the people who had shown such kindness towards us. It wasn't the last thing we received from them either: they used to send us lovely food parcels containing chocolates and other goodies at Christmas time all the way from Canada. These parcels were well received because even though the war was over, there was still a shortage of certain things.

Members of the family would come and stay with us occasionally. I recall eagerly awaiting the arrival of my aunt from Plymouth, and discovering that part of her stay was going to coincide with my trip to the hospital in Newcastle-upon-Tyne to have my tonsils and adenoids removed. I was very nervous on the day I had to go into hospital. I had to wear a rubber cape and thick woollen socks (which I saw some boys sliding along the floor in). When I woke up after the operation, I realised I was back in my bed, with a sore throat and an enamel bowl by the side of my mouth to catch the blood. At first I could not eat solids, but on my final day, just before the expected arrival of my father to take me home, I was given my first normal dinner. My father was later as he had been held up by the tide. I was so relieved to see him and go home, where my mother and aunt were waiting for me.

My uncle Bill Lentell who was in the Navy, made arrangements while his ship was docked in Newcastle-upon-Tyne for a few days to visit St Mary's lighthouse. When the day of his expected arrival came I couldn't wait to see him. The tide was still over the causeway but I had often seen Mr Crisp wade across in his thigh boots and he didn't get wet. And so, with my Wellington boots on, I began to do likewise. I waded out until the water started to rush into my boots, but I decided not to let a little thing like some water in my boots worry me. But by the time I had reached the half way mark between the island and the mainland, the water was up to my neck. My mother began to panic when she noticed where I was, and immediately called my father who pulled on his thigh boots and started to walk after me. He did not shout in case he alarmed me. I finally reached the other side, took off my boots and started to shake the water out of them. I felt very damp and wondered how Mr Crisp managed to stay so dry when he made the crossing. It was at this point that I heard my father saying, "And where do you think you are going, young lady?" To meet Uncle Bill, of course.

Warm pools amongst the rocks, seaweed, rowing boats, and the changing tide were second nature to me but I had a lot to learn about the land. I always remember the first time my mother took me for a walk along the cliffs to the farm. I had my first sight of real chickens, and lots of them. I was so thrilled to see these feathery creatures that I ran among them hoping to catch one and make friends with it. Instead of catching them I was causing them to run in all directions. The farmer's wife came out to see what was causing the disturbance. My mother was very red in the face as she explained her daughter had never seen a chicken before.

St Mary's is a very picturesque island but a mother with small children has a difficult task trying to prevent her children from falling, as there are so many dangerous places. As a result my mother used to tell me it was safer to stay in the garden and play. If I did stray from the garden my mother would be very close behind me to see I didn't get into too much trouble. However, on one occasion my mother made an exception to the rule. A little girl, much older than me, came to stay next door. She looked over the garden wall and invited me for a walk around the island. My mother agreed and all was well until I climbed over a railing and fell down a seven-foot drop. I landed on my back and my mother could hear the screams from our living room. After that, I was not allowed to leave the garden as before.

Since sweets had been in short supply during the war, it was magic to my ears when my mother gave me some money and told me to go down to the newly opened café and buy some chocolate. I was reluctant to go at first because I did not want to leave my new balloon. I was afraid my mother would lose it. She assured me she would look after the balloon until I came back. However, on my way back from the café I saw the balloon flying in a northerly direction towards Blythe. I rushed home and found my parents looking rather sheepish. When I wasn't playing with balloons, I used to like to play mothers and fathers myself. I realised that for this game I had to have an imaginary husband. I decided to call him Butt, in memory of the butts at the firing range.

In order to keep a lighthouse running smoothly, everything has to be immaculate. For instance, my father and the other keepers used to go up the lighthouse daily to clean the lenses and all the working parts in the lantern. Likewise the keepers' houses had to be kept spotlessly clean. To check on the state of the buildings, every so often Trinity House Brethren and the Superintendent for the area would make an inspection of the lighthouse and living quarters.

My mother used to play her part by keeping our house clean and tidy. She was always impressing upon me to play in the lamp room, next to the kitchen, so that my toys would not be strewn about the kitchen floor. One day, as it was rather cold in the lamp room, she made an exception and allowed me to play by the fire in the kitchen. However, on looking out of the window, she could see a group of official-looking people crossing the causeway towards the lighthouse. She immediately asked me to clear my toys away. I threw them on the floor in the lamp room, as there wasn't enough time to put them away. The men arrived at the tower door, and after a tour of the lighthouse they knocked on our front door. They said they were from Trinity House and that they wished to inspect our living quarters; my mother invited them in. When she had finished discussing the business of the day, one of the men turned to me and said, "Where shall we go, Patricia?" I immediately thought of my toys and opened the door to the lamp room, showing him the horrible mess. My mother looked like she wanted to drop through the floor at that moment!

When my father was off-duty he enjoyed several hobbies when not fishing. He gained a lot of satisfaction from making crystal wireless sets and playing the mandolin and violin. He also liked painting lighthouses and seascapes; on one occasion his paintings were accepted at the Laing Art Gallery in Newcastle-upon-Tyne. I was very proud of my father's achievement.

In June 1946, my father received notification from Trinity House that he was to be transferred to Beachy Head lighthouse near Eastbourne, Sussex. This meant that my mother and I would have to move to the Isle of Wight as Beachy Head lighthouse came under the jurisdiction of the Trinity House Depot in East Cowes.

I was initially rather uncertain, as it all seemed rather sudden. I would no longer be able to frequent the places that had become familiar to me. Amidst the fear of encountering a new place and new people, I did have a feeling of excitement, and children at school seemed to regard me with a little more interest than usual, making me feel quite important.

When the removal day finally came on 30th July 1946 and our furniture was moved out I felt as if my world was crumbling around me. My parents knew we were destined for a lodging house in Cowes and that there would be no place for Smut the cat, so he had to be returned to the lady who gave him to us as a kitten. I was heartbroken, but my mother said he was going to a good home.

After our furniture van crossed the causeway, and we had our final wash and brush up, our taxi arrived to transport us to Whitley Bay and the railway station. We crossed the causeway and, as the taxi man drove along the cliff edge, I realised that this was possibly the last time I would see St Mary's lighthouse. I could not bring myself to turn back for a final look. It was time to look ahead to a bright future. After all, the war was behind us and that was something to be thankful for.

10

Trying to put down roots: Beachy Head and Casquets

On 31ˢᵗ July 1946 we arrived on the Isle of Wight after travelling overnight from Northumberland. Unfortunately for us, it was Cowes week, meaning that finding accommodation was going to be an extremely difficult task. We met a lighthouse keeper who kindly took us home for a cup of tea and gave us some reliable addresses. We called on them all but were unsuccessful until we arrived at the final address on the list. Although the lady first shook her head sympathetically, at the sight of our disappointed faces she said, "I wonder if my next door neighbour would be willing to put you up? She doesn't normally take paying guests but she may be willing to help out for a few days, just so you have a roof over your heads until Cowes Week is over". When we called next door, the neighbour kindly welcomed us and agreed to put us up for a few days.

Cowes had grown from a small port in the early nineteenth century to a yachting centre with an international reputation. This began when in 1811, the Duke of Gloucester used to place bets on local craft in unofficial races. This pastime began to appeal to quite a few people, and in 1813 a formal regatta was organised and boats were chartered for the purpose of racing, manned by professional seamen. It wasn't long before the well to-do gentlemen joined in the races and commissioned yachts built solely for pleasure. In 1815 a group of gentlemen met under the organisation of the Honourable Charles Pelham (later Lord Yarborough) at the Thatched House Tavern in St James Street, London to form The Yacht Club, of which there were initially forty-two members. Prospective members had to be of good social standing, own a yacht over a certain tonnage and of course pay an entrance fee. After the club had been in existence for two years the Prince Regent requested to join. When he became King George IV the Club was renamed The Royal Yacht Club. For years it seems nobility have been in the habit of descending on Cowes, especially during Cowes week.

Now that my father was stationed on a rock light he had to spend two months at the lighthouse followed by a month on shore in East Cowes. I looked forward to the days he shared with my mother and I. When the time came for him to return to the lighthouse after a month's leave he had to cross to the mainland from the Isle of Wight to catch the train to Eastbourne, followed by a trip in a small boat to Beachy Head lighthouse. The old 47-feet-high tower, which still stands on the top of the 284-feet-high Belle Tout cliff, was established in 1828. The new tower was built in 1899, 100 feet high, situated 2,200 yards southeast from the old tower.

In September of 1946, I began school in East Cowes. Although my teacher was kind and helpful, my classmates were a little uncertain of me. They referred to me as the 'overner', someone from the mainland. However, after a grass-eating initiation ceremony, I was lucky enough to avoid trouble. I rejoined the Brownies, began piano lessons, learnt to ride a bike, and discovered I enjoyed community singing. I enjoyed the ease of walking to school on the pavement, and not having to consider a tide. I was happy to listen to Just William on the wireless, but sad to be denied the opportunity to hear Dick Barton Special Agent. (My mother read an article in the national press describing the programme – which by today's standards was mild – as disreputable!)

After two months we found furnished rooms with a lady in Yarborough Road. I enjoyed sitting in the front room observing passers-by. Some people passed the window with a smile on their face but, on the other hand, I always felt sad when I saw a small group of German prisoners-of-war pass by. They looked sad and forlorn. I would smile with enthusiasm and hope that it was possible to brighten up their day with a smile. Although my mother was extremely happy with her new landlady, she continued to search for an unfurnished flat or house to rent so she could bring her furniture out of storage in Newport. In fact, my mother put all her energy into searching for accommodation, and became quite stressed. After another six months, however, she found a place to let in West Cowes. It was in a roomy house with a large garden, and the landlord seemed very pleasant. My mother asked him if she could bring my father over to see the flat. My father was due to come ashore for a month's leave beginning the following week. The gentleman agreed, and my mother and I felt very excited about the prospect of seeing our furniture and belongings again.

When my father came home my mother was eager to take him over to see the flat. He said he would have to call in at the Trinity House Depot on his way to check for any possible orders or instructions. My mother waited for him by the chain ferry between East and West Cowes. When he returned he looked rather sombre. "What's the matter?" asked my mother. My father told her that he had received orders to transfer to the Casquets Lighthouse off the Channel Islands on 25th March 1947. My mother felt like crying. After all her efforts to find a flat we would have to move. It meant taking me away from school again, just as I was beginning to settle. It was simply one of those unavoidable changes of plan that servicemen and their families had to endure. When a keeper entered the Trinity House service, he was made aware of the fact that he would have to move from one lighthouse to another when called upon to do so, and it was his decision whether he accepted or not.

The wrench of leaving the Isle of Wight wasn't as great as when leaving St Mary's Island. I had not seen my toys for nine months, and did not have a cat to say goodbye to. My father went over to the Channel Islands before us, and hunted for a guesthouse for us to stay at. We were therefore able to set off with the knowledge that we were assured of accommodation when we arrived at our destination in Alderney. We had heard that our landlady was to be a Miss Louise Mayout. She had apparently made my father very welcome and said she was looking forward to meeting us.

First of all we had to board the ferry at Cowes to cross to Southampton. At Southampton we boarded a ferry destined for Guernsey in the Channel Islands. The sea was very rough, and my mother being a poor sailor spent a lot of the journey being sick. We had not reserved a cabin, and could not do so at such a late stage as they were fully booked. It seemed as if the deck was to be our sleeping place for the journey until the steward kindly took pity on us and allowed us to sleep on the floor of the dining room area. After docking at St Peter's Port in Guernsey, we spent a weekend there before embarking on the final part of our journey to Alderney. At first my mother complained that the floor and ceiling would not stop moving, but she finally got her land-legs back again.

We managed to do a little sightseeing while on Guernsey for the weekend. I remember the Little Chapel at Les Vauxbelets in the parish of St Andrew, possibly the smallest chapel in the world. Apparently Brother Déodat (1878-1951), the sacristan of the nearby Catholic seminary, made it his task to collect all kinds of discarded shards and glass to build a tiny chapel. This unusual building is only large enough to hold four or five people at a time. After the death of Brother Déodat, Brother Cephas worked on the chapel until his retirement in 1965. I have been told that when a china item was broken on Guernsey, housewives would console themselves by saying that it would be something nice for Les Vauxbelets.

After our weekend in Guernsey, we had to board the boat for Alderney, which was going to be my island home for over three years. Before boarding the ferry, I had not appreciated how far we were going to be from the English coast. A passenger told my mother that it was about a hundred miles, although the French coast was only twelve miles away (perhaps that explains why *Aurigny* enjoys about eighteen hundred hours of sunshine a year). The same passenger informed us that apart from the Chausey Islands, which had been assigned to France, the Channel Islands belonged to the British Crown but not the United Kingdom, from which they were independent. They had their own laws, stamps and currency, which varied from island to island. We learned that Alderney was mostly independent of Guernsey, especially where financial and legal matters were concerned. The local residents elected a President and twelve representatives every three years, and the States Parliament members elected a Vice-President every year. However, Guernsey provided the police force. (This status was altered at the end of 1948).

The RMS Queen Elizabeth passing Alderney, painted by Harold Owen in 1949.

We made our way to the guesthouse in the High Street by the name of *Bonjour*. At last we were able to meet Louise, our French landlady of whom we had heard so much. She had white hair and a kind face, and her and my mother formed a close and lasting friendship. I remember how the black lead grate in her fireplace had been polished until you could almost see your face in it. I felt even more at home after meeting her two cats and white mongrel puppy called Georgie Boy. The cats were called Miss Icks and Miss Annie. Poor Miss Icks rolled around as if in a drunken stupor. This amused me until I was told that Miss Icks had been accidentally poisoned during the German occupation.

Louise knew a lot about the history of Casquets lighthouse, my father's new workplace, situated about eight miles northwest of Alderney. Peter Le Measurier, whilst he was Governor of Jersey, had three lighthouses erected there as early as 1785: Donjon on the northeast, St Thomas and St Peter. Apparently before these lighthouses were erected there was scarcely a gale without some ship running aground and being destroyed. In 1870, oil lamps replaced the coal fires. In 1877 only one lighthouse out of the three was still working. She told us how during the nineteenth century one family lived at the lighthouse for eighteen years without leaving. One day a carpenter came to the lighthouse and fell in love with the lighthouse keeper's daughter. She went to Alderney with him but could not stand the noise on the larger island after the isolation of the Casquets. She went back to the Casquets only to return to Alderney to marry her true love. Her father also moved to Alderney. I was pleased I wasn't destined for Casquets and that the light keepers families no longer resided on the tiny island. From what I had seen so far, Alderney was small enough (3 miles long by 1.5 miles wide). The light keepers were taken off the Casquets permanently in 1940 and German troops built a signal station there. However, in 1942 British Commandos stormed the lighthouse and captured the German occupants, retrieving some confidential papers.

My mother arranged for me to start school after a few days of rest. At the time, the one and only school on Alderney was situated in the town of St Ann's and was known as The Town School. The schoolhouse was situated by a bell tower with a sundial and was built by a John Le Measurier in 1790. Being the new girl from England, I had to earn the respect of the local children who were generally friendly. However, there were a few bullies amongst them who gave me a hard time. One or two boys thought it amusing to knock my head against a brick wall. Sometimes, to avoid boredom, they would change the punishment by knocking me off my feet and treading on my hands. Naturally I was rather distressed and the prospect of further harassment from this small group caused me to go home at lunchtime with a tearstained face. I begged my mother to let me stay home from school for the rest of the day. This upset my mother and she was at her wits end to know what to do for the best.

One day I arrived home from school and my mother said she had been having a word with the Catholic Priest who was also resident at *Bonjour* while awaiting the completion of repairs to his Presbytery. Like many other buildings it had suffered damage during the German occupation, but was due to open its doors again. Although we were not Catholics the Priest did not see any reason why my mother should not put my name down to be one of the first pupils to commence lessons when the school reopened.

Every day while I was coping with school my mother walked the streets of Alderney to find a place to live, becoming well acquainted with the cobbled stone streets and colourful houses. My mother and I had a lot to thank Louise for during this time as she cheered my mother up when she returned, disappointed, from her house-hunting expedition and would make me laugh after a depressing school day. Six months had elapsed since we first set foot on the island and much to my mother's delight she found an unfurnished house to let. At long last she would be able to ask for her furniture to be sent over from Newport in the Isle of Wight, which we had not seen for 15 months. Louise was pleased to hear my mother's good news and said that she hoped my mother would visit her regularly. My mother kept her word and eventually Louise referred to herself as my mother's Alderney Mother.

Finally, I was reunited with my dolls and teddy bear. Unfortunately, the only thing missing was my cat, Smut, who used to live with us at St Mary's. My mother could see that I was very keen to have another cat, so when a friend offered me a kitten my mother did not need much persuasion to allow me to take up the offer. It was a pretty marmalade coloured kitten, and we decided to call him Buttons.

Our new home was situated opposite the hospital in Victoria Street. The rooms were spacious with sea views from the sitting room and front bedroom windows. On the top floor were two attic bedrooms, the largest of which my mother designated as my playroom. We had a large dining room downstairs, adjoining the kitchen/scullery that looked out onto a secluded garden.

Not only was I to have a new home but a new school. When I first set foot in the Convent I was overawed by the sight of the nuns, but they were very kind and it did not take them long to gain my confidence. It was a small homely school. I often remember winter days sitting in the classroom with a coal fire blazing away in the grate. At first I took religious instruction at the Convent School, but after a few weeks it was decided that for this lesson the

Protestant schoolchildren should go to the Town School. One of my companions was the daughter of the Trinity House Pilot on Alderney, and when the teacher told us the story of Pontius Pilate, my friend put up her hand and proudly informed us all that her father was also a Pilot, causing uproar!

I made friends with the two daughters of the French chef at the Grand Hotel on The Butes, as they attended the Convent school also. Poor Michelle had badly deformed legs, which she hid under a pair of trousers. My mother thought it was due to a lack of certain foods and vitamins during the war. Michelle and Giselle's father was very keen for them to learn English. One day the Reverend Mother chastised them in impeccable French, telling them that they weren't making a very good attempt at learning English.

While at the Convent, my schoolwork began to improve. Previously, I had experienced a disjointed education through no fault of my own, but in the peaceful surroundings of the Convent I seemed to make a noticeable improvement, and one day was so proud when my teacher suggested I be put up a class. It gave me encouragement to work even harder. I was also enthusiastic when it came to school plays, and one year I was chosen to be Rip Van Winkle. I remember that there weren't enough props to go around, and as a result I had to share a beard with another boy. He didn't bring me the beard when he came off stage and as I was rather nervous about my first entry, I forgot to ask him for it. I went on stage with legs trembling, and as I started to deliver my lines, heard from the wings a voice saying, "Oh dear, Patricia has forgotten her beard".

The Convent School building, which was situated in the secluded and peaceful Royal Connaught Square, had at one time been known as Government House. Due to the fact that it was not all that long after the end of the Second World War and German occupation of Alderney, there were still statues of Saints without heads and arms as well as paintings on walls with a German theme. Work on restoring the building to its original state had only begun at the same time as the opening of the Convent School. There was a number of German prisoners-of-war in Alderney, clearing up the mess. One by the name of Francis was detailed to sort things out in the Convent. He was very fond of children and when he saw me he picked me up, much to my alarm. The priest assured my mother that Francis was a very good catholic and we had no need to fear him.

I was glad I was not on Alderney in 1940 because the Channel Islands were demilitarised and its inhabitants advised to stay calm and not to resist in the event of an invasion by German troops. The islanders naturally thought they had been betrayed but the decision was made in an effort to save them from destruction. Ten days before German troops arrived there was great confusion. The farm animals were neglected and pets roamed the streets while inhabitants tried to decide whether or not to stay. The British Navy evacuated those that decided to leave Alderney. In their haste to leave, people buried their valuables. On 3rd July, Alderney was occupied and some of the Germans thought they had landed on the Isle of Wight or the south coast of England.

After two years, food became scarce and fishermen could not go out in their boats very often as the waters around the islands were mined. Prices of groceries such as tea and butter had risen out of control on the 'black market'. The Germans finally issued an order that all residents between the ages of sixteen and seventy who weren't natives of the island should be deported. They were transported by ship to camps in Germany.

The island forts which had been in existence since before the Napoleonic times were modified to suit the needs of the Germans as protection against Britain between 1940 and 1945. There were about thirteen of those around the island of Alderney. For added protection, and so as not to be seen by our aircraft, the Germans dug passageways under the ground in several parts of the island and knocked holes between the terraced houses in the streets, thus enabling them to walk unobserved from one end of the street to the other.

Wirelesses were banned in 1942, but islanders managed to hide a few sets to keep themselves informed about the progress of the war. During the winter of 1944, the weather was bitterly cold. Morale was low and starvation seemed inevitable. Around about November a fisherman, together with an accomplice, asked for permission to take a boat out to do some crab fishing. He pretended the boat needed some repairs in St Peter's Port, Guernsey, but instead of heading for Guernsey he tried to head for France to get help from the Red Cross. Apparently an American destroyer picked him up 50 nautical miles south of Guernsey.

On December 27th a Red Cross ship delivered food supplies, and on May 8th 1945 at 10:00 the Bailiffs of Jersey and Guernsey were informed by the Germans that the war was over and that the British flag could be hoisted. On the same day Winston Churchill gave his Victory-Day speech. On 9th May the peace documents were signed. British destroyers, which had been guarding the Channel, set sail for the islands. There followed scenes of great joy.

After a farewell concert given by the Germans for the islanders at a prison camp where they presented works by Beethoven, Mozart and Chopin, they returned home to Germany on good terms with the islanders. When the evacuated islanders began to return they found their furniture and belongings missing. When my family and I first arrived on Alderney in 1947 we heard tales of people afraid to ask friends into their houses for fear their friends would recognise items of their own furniture.

One evening when my mother and I were out for a stroll we walked into a derelict concentration camp, which was fenced off behind barbed wire. During spells of childhood curiosity I explored the underground passageways built in hills near The Butes by the Germans. My mother was always warning me of the perils of such pastimes. The tunnels were shored up with wood, but the wood was in a bad state of repair. I had an uneasy feeling one time while crawling through a tunnel, and made an immediate exit through a spy hole. A few days later I plucked up enough courage to return, only to find the tunnel had caved in.

During the summer months my mother took me to the beach, but much to my disappointment she favoured the isolation of Longy Bay on the east coast of Alderney. Although I preferred Braye beach, as there were other children there that I could play with, my mother had got so used to the remoteness of St Mary's Lighthouse that she needed a little time on her own. However, if I went to Alderney today, I think I too would head for Longy Bay, as it is interesting from a historical point of view. There is a fort at one end of Longy Bay called Essex Castle. Apparently, Essex Castle had its beginnings in 1547 as a citadel. It was then known as *Les Murs de Hant*. When John Chamberlain was Governor of the Island he sold the castle for £1,000 to Robert Devereux, Earl of Essex, who was an admirer of Queen Elizabeth I. He was condemned to death for high treason in 1601 and it is thought that he never visited Alderney. The castle was built in the middle of the nineteenth century on the ruins of the old fort. Legend has it that at midnight on New Year's Eve a little man is supposed to step out of a cupboard in the tower, make three turns round the tower, and disappear for another twelve months. There is also an island off Longy Bay, which can be reached by causeway at low tide, on which sits the fort *Ile de Raz* known originally as *Le Houmet de Longis*.

As I grew older I became more adventurous and there were several occasions I walked down to Braye Beach alone and climbed up onto the roof of the derelict stone houses. They were three or four storeys high and when I reached the top I could look at the ground through broken girders on the other side of the wall, although I felt a little uncertain about my safety. I seemed to be fearless then! The beach was strewn with broken china left over from the occupation, and one day I received a painful cut on the ball of my foot. While I sat on the beach nursing my wound I looked over towards Fort Albert. It was named after Queen Victoria's husband Prince Albert. The Fort was built in 1886, equipped with a cannon, and used as a military headquarters until 1929. The Germans, in 1940, made the building their main defence position as it stood on the north side of the island and presented them with a good view of the Channel and the mainland of France.

One Sunday afternoon my mother and I went for a walk to Fort Clonque. The name was apparently derived from the French *calanque* meaning rocky inlet. A causeway had been built to link the fort, built in 1854 on Ortac Rock, with the rest of the island. It was said that the spirit who controlled the wind and weather lived there, who the sailors used to drink to in an attempt to appease. This belief developed from the existence of a dangerous current referred to as 'The Swinge', which caught many ships off guard.

On Sundays most of my friends went to the Catholic Church. I, on the other hand, went to St Ann's Church in Victoria Street. The church was designed by Sir George Gilbert Scott and was built of Caen stone and Alderney sandstone. It was consecrated in 1850, and there is a church register going back to 1662. When the Germans occupied the island the church was used as a warehouse. The bells were taken down and hidden in France. They were found in Cherbourg after the war ended.

When we lived on Alderney they did not have a rating system. As a result the dustman used to charge us 6d every time he came to empty our dustbin. I recall that he looked like he had all the cares of the world on his shoulders, hence the nickname 'Happy'. Road sweepers were non-existent so all residents, my mother and staff at the hospital opposite included, had to sweep the pavement outside the front door and half way across the road. Every night at midnight the streetlights would go out. It was at this time that we would hear the hospital generators being switched on and see the lights being turned on in the hospital. Whenever we heard a hand-bell being rung, we would make a dash for the front door so that we could hear what the Town Crier had to say.

My mother and I, more often than not, spent Christmas quietly on our own. However, I was very excited one Christmas as it was my father's turn to be ashore. On Christmas Eve he arrived home but unfortunately he was recalled to Casquets lighthouse on Boxing Day, as one of his work mates was very ill with pneumonia. He was brought ashore and taken to the hospital across the road from us. When permitted to have visitors, my mother and I went over to see him. Nevertheless, I found Christmas and New Year on Alderney very enjoyable. The fire brigade would assemble in Marais Square on

Christmas morning, and anyone who was brave enough to walk through the square risked a soaking from the hoses or a ducking in the cattle trough.

My father's New Year resolution one year was to do more gardening. He decided to turn the earth over and get rid of the weeds. He was so surprised to discover a box containing silver objects. After carefully cleaning the silver we found the name of the owner inscribed on each item, and so we were able to return it all. As a token of thanks, the owner invited us to tea and gave us some newly laid eggs for our breakfast the next day.

My hobby was hoarding royal memorabilia. I collected books on the Royal Family and spent hours looking at the pictures and reading the comments underneath. I also made scrapbooks of the Royal Family, neatly cutting the pictures and pasting them in, ensuring they were in chronological order. For Christmas 1948, my grandmother sent me a book about the Royal Wedding of Princess Elizabeth and Prince Philip, which took place on Thursday 20th November 1947 in Westminster Abbey in London. I was over the moon when I heard the royal couple were to visit the Channel Islands in June 1949, beginning in Alderney on Tuesday 21st. But our trip to my father's family in Plymouth had to coincide with my father's leave from Casquets lighthouse, and we left Alderney a few days before the royal couple arrived. I was devastated.

After my mother's traumatic sea journey on her way out to the Channel Islands, she decided we would fly. Our plane was a seven-seated twin-engine biplane known as a *De Havilland Rapide*. This was a new and thrilling experience for me, rising above the small white clouds with occasional glimpses of the water below. My mother looked up at the emergency exit and back to her own waistline and hoped we did not have the need to make a sudden exit. We flew over the Needles lighthouse off the Isle of Wight. My father was stationed on the Needles as a young man so he was excited to see it from the air. Needles lighthouse was erected by Trinity House in 1859 and built from granite at a height of 109 feet. I thought it looked majestic against the background of the white cliffs, blue sea and the green fields. In seconds we were flying over the mainland with the patchwork green fields and winding roads. Eventually Eastleigh Airport came in to sight, and after landing we were greeted by a Customs Officer. We had nothing to declare, and were soon on our way by taxi towards the nearest Railway Station and the train bound for Plymouth.

I always looked forward to going to Plymouth as there was always plenty to do and the bustle of city life was welcome after spending such a lot of time in various isolated corners of the British Isles. Plymouth was being raised out of the dust with amazing speed and everyone seemed determined to get back to normal after the devastation created by wartime raids. Aunt Anne, Uncle Dan and Grandad always gave us such warm welcomes. Grandad would let me listen to Dick Barton Special Agent. Uncle John (my father's brother), Aunt Dollie and cousin John would often come up from Cornwall to see us. I looked on my cousin as the nearest thing to a brother, as I always wished to be one of a large family. We also took the opportunity to visit Aunt Maud and Uncle Bill (my father's sister and brother-in-law). At times I could persuade Uncle Bill to relate some of his hair-raising sea stories.

Finally, our holiday came to an end and we returned to Alderney. When my Aunt wrote to reply to our thank you letter she said that the Royal couple were due to visit Plymouth. I had missed them twice!

After that trip to Plymouth we lived on Alderney for another twelve months before my father received orders to transfer to St Ann's Head lighthouse, near the village of Dale and the town of Milford Haven in Pembrokeshire. The transfer date was 29th May 1950.

The nuns at the Convent School were sorry to learn of my forthcoming departure from their school. They told my mother that it would be beneficial for me to stay as a boarder, as I was picking up so well. My mother gave it some thought but she preferred us to be together.

While my father was serving his final month on Casquets lighthouse, my mother was busy packing all our belongings into tea chests and, with my help, rolling up carpets and linoleum. It was extremely distressing to have to say goodbye to Buttons as well as all our other friends. As Alderney was such a small island, we knew most of the people there and felt that we had become one of them.

11

Together at St Ann's Head lighthouse

My mother always had a soft spot for Wales so the prospect of living there again pleased her, although she was sad to wave goodbye to Alderney. She knew she would now have plenty of opportunities to visit her mother who lived twenty-one miles from St Ann's lighthouse, in a little place called Neyland. My grandmother and grandfather moved to the area when my mother was twelve and her sister, Aunt May, was six. Their brother, Uncle Bill, also moved to the area at the same time but had since moved away. He was a seafaring man like his father and had attended the Royal Naval College at Greenwich.

We travelled from Alderney to St Ann's by plane, train and finally taxi. St Ann's Head is on the tip of Dale Peninsula, sheltering the entrance to Milford Haven from westerly gales, of which St Ann's certainly has its fair share. They sometimes gust to 90 mph and 31.5 days of gales have been recorded in one year. In pre-glacial times the sea ran through the Dale Valley and the St Ann's peninsular was an island. The strait was eventually filled with material released from the melting ice. However, the wind, waves and rain are gradually causing this material to be eroded away.

On the topic of lighthouses, my father knew a lot of history. He told me how the very first lighthouse, the Pharos lighthouse, was situated at the port of Alexandria in Egypt. In 1600 there was only one lighthouse on the whole coast of Britain but by 1700 there were fourteen, and 1819, thirty-seven. In addition to the present lighthouse at St Ann's Head, at which my father served, there is the old lighthouse, which is no longer in use. This particular lighthouse, built around 1662, was the first lighthouse to be built on the Welsh coast.

Several generations of my father's family have served at St Ann's lighthouse. My father's great grandfather John Hall who was born in Dale, commenced duties for Trinity House at St Ann's and finally died in Holyhead, North Wales. My father's grandfather, Thomas Owen Hall, was born in Dale at the Post Office and died at Flamborough lighthouse.

My mother had her own memories of St Ann's Head. On 16ᵗʰ July 1933, she sat in a boat while my father swam from St Ann's Head to Pembroke

Dock. It took him four hours and twenty minutes to complete the swim. My mother was most likely feeling very cold after sitting in the boat all that time, but I think my father must have been feeling exhausted. When he eventually pulled himself out of the water at Pembroke Dock and walked up the beach, he met an acquaintance who asked him if he had been for a swim. "Yes", was all that my father replied, not mentioning that he had just completed a swim from St Ann's Head. Modesty was always one of his virtues.

When I used to stand on the Head and look out to sea towards the northwest I could see the island of Skokholm. This island was made famous by R M Lockley's books in the thirties. In 1939 Skokholm became the first bird observatory in Britain. People used to go out for a week at a time to observe the birds. The West Wales Naturalist Trust and Dale Fort Field Centre currently administer the island. The Edward Grey Institute of Oxford University has a long-standing research programme studying the population of manx shearwaters, storm petrels and other seabirds. After I looked out towards Skokholm for a while I would turn my head around and gaze out towards the other side of the river. I could see a little place called Angle. The name, I believe, comes from a Norse word meaning a corner or turning, which in this case was into the Haven from the open sea. After looking at Angle I would turn around to look at Milford Haven. I always remember people describing Milford Haven as one of the world's finest natural harbours. Today, Milford Haven is an international oil port but when my father, mother and I lived at St Ann's Head from 1950 to 1952, the fishing industry was the main source of employment.

St Ann's was one mile south, where the Royal Naval Direction Centre, HMS *Harrier* was located. The centre is no longer in existence, instead the ground is owned by the National Trust. The coast guard station lay just a few hundred yards to the north of the lighthouse, with adjoining dwellings to house one or two naval personnel from the Royal Naval Camp. The old lighthouse, the coast guard lookout post, and the fog horn were a stone's throw away from the new St Ann's lighthouse and our dwellings. (I was not happy when I realised there was a fog horn although I doubt that the local seamen shared my attitude. When sounded on foggy nights, I found the noise so unbearable that I would be found with my head under the bedclothes with my fingers in my ears, thinking how happy I would be if only fog could be banned forever.)

The new lighthouse had a short tower, and at the side of it were situated the keepers' dwellings. Our dwellings were light and airy, providing fine views of the shipping and trawlers as they made their way into harbour, sometimes fighting their way through rough seas. There were three bedrooms, a sitting room, dining room and a kitchen. I liked the red quarry tiles in the kitchen, which would sparkle after my mother had finished polishing them. There was a small garden at the back of the house, surrounded by a whitewashed wall. If the weather was rough my mother could not hang out her washing for fear of it being blown away or ripped to shreds in the wind. We did, however, experience some nice days, when my mother would get her washing dry in no time at all.

Slightly north of the houses were situated the light keepers' allotments. Quite a few vegetables were grown there, but one year my father decided to cut his smoking bill. (Due to the then annual increases of tax on tobacco, there was a surge of interest in growing your own.) My father planted tobacco plants, and at the same time purchased a manual giving instructions on the complicated process of curing tobacco. It was so complicated, however, that my father gave it up as a bad job and reverted to vegetable growing. There was a limit to the type of plants one could grow there due to the exposed location.

The lighthouse and keepers' residences at St Ann's.
Photograph courtesy of Squibbs of Tenby.

St Ann's lighthouse.

After I had explored the Head thoroughly I decided that it had great potential as far as imaginative games were concerned but I had to make an effort to cope with the feeling of being a long way from the town and life. However, if I lived there today I would probably appreciate that very isolation. But like it or not, I was going to have to adapt to my surroundings – it wasn't as if Alderney was a metropolis.

My mother made arrangements for me to start school at Dale, and my long-prayed-for bike was purchased out of necessity. My mother knew that when I eventually attended secondary school in Milford Haven I would have to cycle into Dale to catch the bus. For the time being there was a taxi available to transport me the three miles into the village school.

The village children were friendly and welcomed me into their midst. I wasn't at the village school for many months before transferring to the secondary school in Milford Haven. I looked forward to the day with mixed feelings. It meant going to a bigger school, and the thought of leaving early in the morning did not appeal to me much. I did, however, like the idea of going into a town and seeing a little bit of life. Life at St Ann's Head was very quiet, especially when one did not own a car. The day finally came and at 07:30 I set off from St Ann's lighthouse on my bicycle to cycle three miles into Dale. I then left my bike at a prearranged spot and boarded the school bus at the Griffin Public House at 8 o'clock prompt. The early departure was necessary because we had to go to the surrounding villages such as Marloes and St Ishmaels. While on the bus, although I was feeling quite smart in my new school uniform, I was conscious of the other more established travellers weighing me up.

When I arrived at school it seemed huge in comparison with anything I had ever experienced before, and after a test it was determined that I should enter the 'A' stream. It wasn't very long before I settled down and I knew I was going to like my new life as a Milford Haven schoolgirl. At first, until my classmates got to know me, I was regarded as something of an oddity, being English and living on a lighthouse.

I found my first day extremely tiring and was relieved when it was time to return to the school bus even if one couldn't hear oneself think. The noise was ear shattering. I never knew how the bus driver survived it. When, finally, the bus arrived outside the Griffin Public House in Dale at 5 o'clock, I called for my bike and started to cycle home with my friends. When we reached Drift Hill it was so steep we had to jump off our bikes and push them up the hill. When we reached the top, we were able to remount and continue on our way, past a pig farm and on towards the gate of my friend's farm where we waved goodbye. We carried on our way past the Naval Camp, where the road turned in a southerly direction for about a mile to the coast guard station and lighthouse. When we reached the coast guard station I waved goodbye to my other companion and cycled the final few hundred yards to the lighthouse dwellings where I could see my mother waving at me through the dining room window. By this time it was approximately half past five. When I arrived in the house my first task was to change out of my uniform and wash and prepare for tea. It was reassuring to be within the refuge of my house, and the problems of the day seemed much less significant when shared with Mother and Father.

After tea I would start on my homework, and by 9 o'clock I would be found climbing the stairs with an oil lamp in my hand. It was a comforting feeling to enter the familiar surroundings of my bedroom with my favourite few ornaments on the mantelpiece. In the centre was my wooden moneybox with a painting of St Mary's lighthouse, serving as a constant reminder of my Northumberland home. These little reminders of my past stopped me from losing my identity, important when I didn't have the security of living in one place all my life.

I don't think my mother was happy about my means of travelling to school as winter descended upon us. She could not see why the education authorities could not provide a taxi for the secondary school children as they had done for the younger children when they attended the Dale village primary school. Her fears were endorsed one morning when, not long after I had left, she watched me cycle past a section of cliff known as the Vomit. A sudden gust of wind blew me off my bicycle, at the same time scattering my schoolbooks about the headland. My coat sleeve was caught in one of the handlebars, thus making it difficult for me to free myself and get up off the ground. As my mother was witnessing this from the bedroom window, she became rather distressed as she thought my failure to get up again in a hurry meant that I had been injured in some way. She was relieved when finally I picked myself up, dusted my uniform down, and ran after my wind-blown and rain soaked books.

After that incident my mother made an appointment to see the education officer, to coincide with one of her weekly trips into Haverfordwest. Trinity House provided a taxi every Wednesday for keepers and families to get food provisions and other requirements. When my mother finally came face to face with the education officer, she explained to him how it would be impossible for me to get to school when winds sometimes gusted to 90 mph. She pointed out that if a strong man like my father had to crawl towards the lighthouse on hands and knees during a gale, there wasn't much hope for a slip of a girl on a bicycle. The officer was sympathetic, but said he could not give her an immediate answer, as it would have to be put before a committee meeting. He said he would let her know the result as soon as he possibly could. We had no telephone then, but were overjoyed when a message was received from the education authorities (via the coast guard) that a taxi was to be provided for children from the lighthouse, coast guard station and surrounding farms to catch their school bus at 8 o'clock each morning in Dale. Everyone congratulated my mother on her success!

On one occasion, however, a motorcyclist rode into our taxi at speed, and pushed us into the hedge. My companion from the coast guard station had a cut finger, but apart from that we were unhurt. If there had been someone in the front passenger seat they would not have been so fortunate. The front window was smashed and most of the glass found its way onto the front seat. Our driver, a local pig farmer, was shocked into silence, and we all felt lucky to be in one piece. My friend's father from the farm brought his lorry, and as the school bus had already left the village of Dale, drove on to intercept the bus. We arrived at school shaken but not hurt. My only concern was my mother who I hoped would not find out about the crash from another source, and worry unnecessarily. When I arrived home later that day, however, I was the first to relate the incident to her.

When I first went to secondary school it took a while to get to know all the rules and regulations and one day I unwittingly broke a rule by walking along a path for boys only. It was my first time in trouble, and I was so scared I started to pull a funny face, which the headmistress interpreted as a disrespectful grin. Luckily I had the sense to apologise later. I enjoyed most lessons in school, not least of all history. I also had a certain appreciation for music and soon found my way into the school choir. I practised with enthusiasm for school concerts, which sadly I could never attend due to the distance and practically non-existent bus service. Since going home at midday was also out of the question, I went to the school canteen. During the summer months, the teachers took us for swimming lessons at the outdoor pool in Milford Haven. Preparing for swimming galas was a sign that the summer vacation was around the corner. I looked forward to the prospect of not having to get up so early in the morning to be ready for the school taxi...bliss!

Milford Haven itself is neat and organised with streets laid out in a gridiron pattern, being one of the few 'planned' towns in South Wales. Work on the town began in 1810 when Quaker Nantucket whalers visited. 1863 saw the railway come into existence, and in 1888 the docks appeared. Trawlers became almost the sole support of the town. If I wasn't browsing around the local shops I was to be found walking along Hamilton Terrace and past the Nelson Hotel during lunch breaks. Apparently Lord Nelson once laid a foundation stone at a local church and delivered a speech, praising the Haven, at a dinner at the hotel.

During the school holidays my mother used to accompany me to Mill Bay for a swim. Mill Bay lies to the northeast of St Ann's lighthouse, past the allotments and Trinity House steps (built so that stores could be delivered to the old lighthouse). More often than not we had the beach to ourselves and I used to swim for hours, gaining a nice golden tan. I did not realise at the time that I was standing on such an historical piece of beach. It is thought that Henry Tudor landed there on 7th August 1485, fifteen days before gaining victory at Bosworth.

During my time at St Ann's Head, a local farmer stored bales of hay in the old lighthouse that used to belong to Trinity House. We were often to be found playing around the base of the building, in some fantasy world, for example having concerts with potato boxes built up on top of one another to form a stage. Naval officers sometimes lived on the Head, and I recall when one of their sons, a Pakistani boy, once came to play with us. He brought his alarm clock with him to remind him when to go home for lunch. We encouraged him to sing some of his native songs. Sometimes he would be in the middle of one when his alarm bell would start to ring and he would immediately stop the ringing and head for home. Some summer evenings we whiled the time away attempting to master the art of cricket. We were always losing cricket balls over the cliff, and eventually our lack of cricket balls stopped play.

The lighthouse keepers and coast guards with both sets of families were given an open invitation to attend the cinema at the naval camp, HMS *Harrier*. We used to walk up to the camp on a Friday evening to see which film was being shown. One evening we watched a thunderstorm on the screen, and when we emerged to begin our walk down the road towards the lighthouse we were faced with a real, live thunderstorm. The mile down the road, between the hedges and telegraph poles, seemed longer than usual. We were understandably relieved to reach the safety of home and the lighthouse. This was not the case on a fine moonlit night. We watched the beam from the lighthouse and the moonlit silvery sea beyond. It always made me think of a particular moonlit night at St Mary's lighthouse after an air raid. I certainly did not want to return to those days.

When harvest time came round I would be found at my friend's farm partaking in the hard work and fun. Her mother made a wonderful tea as reward afterwards: what lovely thick rashers of bacon! I loved seeing the men enjoying their well-deserved meal while discussing farming tactics. They even admitted, between mouthfuls, that my friend could offer them some advice on farming. They would say, "Val's right, you know". I enjoyed walking out with my friend to feed the animals – this is really living, I used to tell myself. Eventually the time came for me to get on my bicycle and head for home with the contented feeling of a happy day well spent.

As the autumn and winter days came upon us I settled indoors to read and make my scrap books of film stars and the royal family. Stamp collecting was another of my favourite pastimes. It was easy for the family to know what to send me for Christmas.

Whenever I was on holiday from school I had the opportunity of travelling to Haverfordwest in the taxi provided on Wednesdays. Haverfordwest interested me with its stuccoed houses and castle on the hill. I enjoyed browsing around the shops with my mother. Whenever we went into the draper's I was fascinated by the lady assistants, dressed in black with immaculate hair, red nails and flashing jewellery on their fingers and wrists. While in Haverfordwest I sometimes heard people speaking in Welsh, usually by the older generation. I always longed to know what they were saying.

Sometimes my mother would combine her trip to Haverfordwest with a trip to Neyland by bus so that we could have lunch with my grandmother and catch the next bus back in time for the taxi back to the lighthouse. As well as our occasional day trips to see my grandmother, my mother and I would spend a long weekend at her bungalow. Neyland was another fascinating town with long terraces of nineteenth-century cottages on the hillside, all so immaculate. Neyland came into being in 1856 as the Atlantic terminus of the Manchester railway. My grandmother used to live in a bungalow just outside Neyland at a place called Llanstadwell, and when I climbed to the top of her back garden I could sit on the seat and have a good view over the river towards Pembroke Dock. There was once a dockyard at Pembroke Dock but it was closed in 1920. I used to enjoy watching the Sunderland flying boats taking off and landing. I had a very clear view of the oil tanks at Pembroke Dock. Apparently they were bombed during the Second World War and were on fire for three weeks with a jet of oil 300 feet high.

It was lovely to have, for once, a regular opportunity to see our family. When one is travelling around the country from one place to another, they can seem very far away. Although I gained in that travel can broaden the mind and provide a better understanding of other people, I often feel I lost out in not being able to spend more time with our families in Neyland and in Plymouth.

On one of our weekend visits to Neyland, my mother agreed to take me over to the seaside resort of Tenby for the day. Tenby has a lovely sandy beach.

I believe in 1566 the population was barely 800 and by the end of the eighteenth century it was almost entirely deserted until 1800 when it became a favoured resort by the upper classes. Tenby is surrounded by walls and has a Norman Castle with Five Arches, although architecturally it is predominantly Regency style. I found it a most pleasant resort to visit and enjoyed my donkey rides along the sands.

Life could sometimes get a little monotonous on St Ann's Head so I was glad to have girlfriends to visit. One weekend comes to mind when I cycled over to Little Haven for the day. My friend had a pony and gave me the chance to ride on the sands. At first I was uncertain and wondered why the pony kept walking into the water, but as soon as my friend taught me how to restrain it from doing so, I enjoyed the ride.

I thought the summer holidays would never end, but unfortunately they did and it was time to go back to school again – which meant homework! The thought of homework made me frown until my mother recited the limerick entitled 'Smile'. By the time she reached the end I started to laugh and decided not to let my work get me down. After all, I was now entering 4th Year at school, and I had to act my age! During the first few weeks of the term I was introduced to shorthand and typing. I realised I would have to persevere with these subjects, and the teacher seemed to have more faith in me than I had in myself.

When my father was informed that he had been promoted to Principal Keeper of the Smalls lighthouse, we had to make rapid arrangements to move. My mother had to inform the school of my imminent departure and the Headmistress very kindly asked me into her office for a cup of tea on my last day at school. I was a deputy prefect and was pleasantly surprised when the headmistress told me that she was sad to see me go and had hoped to eventually promote me to Head Prefect. I felt honoured to be asked into her office for tea, even more so when she told me of her plans to promote me. I thanked her and all my teachers for all they had done for me during my stay in the school.

Although the Smalls Lighthouse is situated approximately nineteen miles off the Milford Haven River, the families had to move to Holyhead because Smalls came under the jurisdiction of the Trinity House Depot there. Smalls lighthouse was first erected on oak piles in 1772, reconstructed in 1778 and rebuilt in 1885, the present stone structure standing at a height of 134.5 feet. When my father moved there the lighthouse was painted red with white bands.

We left St Ann's Lighthouse on 15th October 1952. The removal men had finished moving our furniture by early afternoon. We caught a taxi, waved goodbye, and sped towards town to board the first available train. I had been very happy during my short stay in Pembrokeshire and at the school in Milford Haven. I hoped Holyhead would prove to be as enjoyable to live in. If only, I thought to myself, I had a crystal ball to see what the future had in store for me.

12

Grown-up in Holyhead: Smalls, S. Bishop, Holyhead Breakwater

My father told me to look forward to a breathtaking view before we crossed over to the Isle of Anglesey. I certainly wasn't disappointed. When, from the train, I could see the beautiful Thomas Telford suspension bridge come into view, I agreed with the books that have described it as a masterpiece in design, known as the Gateway to Anglesey. I wished at that moment that I could have been travelling by road so I could have the pleasure of travelling across the bridge. Instead, we were fast approaching Robert Stephenson's Britannia tubular railway bridge, a bridge of equal excellence, guarded at the entrance by two impressive stone lions. When we entered the tunnel we were plunged into darkness and were unable to see the suspension bridge any longer.

We drew into Llanfair-PG, or to give it its proper title, Llanfairpwll-gwyngyllgogerychwyrndrobwll-llantysiliogogogoch, which roughly translated means 'The Church of St Mary in the hollow of white hazel near to the rapid whirlpool of Llandysilio of the red cave'. We crossed the Stanley Embankment, which transports us from the main island of Anglesey to the smaller Holy Island. Holyhead station was not only the end of our journey, but also the end of the railway line. Travellers heading for the Emerald Isle, however, still had a ferry journey ahead of them. Our temporary home was a boarding house ran by a motherly Welsh lady named Mrs Hughes. I remember being aware that most of the people were speaking in Welsh.

The scenery on the Isle of Anglesey is very different to that of the mountainous countryside of Caernarfonshire. It consists of wonderful moors and a rugged coastline, and Holy Island has an average of 1550 hours of sunshine recorded each year. The westerly winds are quite strong, evident in the few wind-sculpted trees that exist on the island. Holyhead 'Mountain' does offer the town of Holyhead some protection from the winds, however. On the northwest coast of Holy Island are situated North Stack and South Stack. Caves below the North Stack provide a home for many sea birds. One mile away, South Stack lighthouse stands on a small island that can be reached by descending about four hundred steps and crossing a chain bridge spanning a narrow channel.

Not far from South Stack Lighthouse stands Holyhead 'Mountain', only 720 feet high. From the top, one can look out to the Irish Sea and Ireland beyond. On a clear day, the Mountains of Mourne and the Wicklow Hills can be seen. In the opposite direction, the Snowdonia Mountain range is visible.

While we were still living in South Wales, King George sadly passed away on 6th February 1952. The coronation of our present Queen, Elizabeth II, took place on 2nd June 1953 at Westminster Abbey, not long after we had moved into our rented accommodation in Walthew Avenue in Holyhead. A friend from school kindly invited me to her house to watch the ceremony on television. I watched the pageantry with great delight, but the moment that will always dwell in my mind is when the Archbishop placed the crown upon the Queen's head followed immediately by the cries of "God Save the Queen".

My new school, Holyhead County, was celebrating its 50th anniversary in 1953. When I first joined the school, I became a member of the Music Society. One of my first tasks was to learn the school song in Welsh and English. I enjoyed practising for my first concert with them. We performed Purcell's opera "Dido and Aeneas". We received a favourable write-up in the June edition of the School Magazine. The school staff had decided to send a copy of this edition to the Queen as her Coronation coincided with our fiftieth anniversary.

While I was at school my mother resumed her usual task of looking for a house to rent. One day when on my way home with a friend I took a detour to explore the road running parallel with Walthew Avenue. I saw an empty bungalow and took the liberty of calling on the owner of the property who resided a few houses away in the next road. I made arrangements for my mother to meet the owner. Before long before our furniture van was at the door to move us in.

After my father completed a short spell at the Smalls lighthouse he was transferred to South Bishop lighthouse (12 miles east of Smalls), and he found that his six years of duty there as an Assistant Keeper before he met my mother were a great help to him as a Principal. The South Bishop lighthouse, which can be seen from Whitesand Bay near St David's Head in Pembrokeshire, was completed in 1839. It is only 36 feet in height although it stands 144 feet above the high water mark. My father used to say that during clear weather, he could see as far as the Irish coast.

During my father's time at Smalls lighthouse, there was one occasion when he had to depart in a great hurry due to ill health. He was suffering from food poisoning and at first thought it was nothing serious, but it soon became obvious he needed medical attention. He was forced to send an R/T message to the superintendent at Holyhead, who made arrangements to bring him ashore. When the Medical Officer examined him he said, "You nearly left it too late, old man". The result was that he was very ill for a week or two.

Smalls lighthouse, where my father worked as Principal Keeper in 1953.

We remained at Holyhead, and he continued to live on the lighthouse for two months followed by one month ashore. It was always great to see him and pass on the latest news. Our home always seemed slightly hollow when, once more, my father returned to the lighthouse. My mother had to take on the role of running the bungalow and being both mother and father to me. It couldn't have been easy but she never complained.

During this time I was working very hard preparing for my school-leaving certificate. I supplemented my school studies with evening classes, in order to gain a pass. On achieving my certificate, my father gave me one of his paintings, entitled 'Sea and Air' which I still have in my possession today. The painting depicts a Sunderland Flying Boat flying past the mouth of the river (which eventually leads up to Milford Haven and Pembroke Dock) from St Ann's Head. By the height of the plane it appears as if it is preparing to land at Pembroke Dock.

'Sea and Air', painted by my father in 1950, a present for gaining my school-leaving certificate.

I left school in July 1955 and in September began work as a junior secretary with a Holyhead Solicitor. I worked there for 18 months until March 1957 when I took up a post as secretary to a Mr Pollecoff, who owned several department stores in the area. I was based at the then Holyhead branch. I was extremely content, having many hobbies and pastimes. During my leisure time I enjoyed ballroom dancing, theatre and cinema, collecting records, cycling and sightseeing whenever possible.

My father transferred yet again, this time to the lighthouse on the end of Holyhead breakwater. We continued to live in our rented bungalow at Holyhead and my father was able to pop in and see us every third day when he came into town to collect his groceries. We were thankful that, at least for the time being, he didn't have to go off to a rock light for two months at a time.

Breakwater lighthouse at Holyhead, my father's final posting before we left North Wales in 1959.

However in August 1959, my father was informed that he was to be transferred to the rock station of Beachy Head lighthouse off the Sussex coast. This wasn't the first time for him to be stationed there, as he served at Beachy Head for 9 months in 1946. I helped my mother pack up the furniture ready for the removal van and I had the sad task of saying goodbye to all the dear friends I had made during my stay in North Wales. My friend from Llanfachraeth and I laughed together when we recalled the time I first went out by bus to see her. I spent hours beforehand learning how to say Llanfachraeth so that I could make the bus conductor understand where I wished to go. I knew that I would remember my friends for many years to come.

We left Holyhead in September 1959. Once again we were to wave goodbye to the furniture van, as it disappeared around the corner with our furniture stacked neatly inside. It was destined for the furniture store in Newport on the Isle of Wight once more.

Ffarwel Cymru.

13

Completing the circuit: Beachy Head and St Mary's Island

After a night on the train and a trip on the Portsmouth to Ryde ferry, we arrived at the Isle of Wight. We had been recommended to a landlady in Ryde, and arrived on her doorstep at 11 o'clock in the morning. She invited us in, told us where to take our suitcases, and offered us a welcome cup of tea. We had booked bed and breakfast and evening meal, so after drinking the cup of tea we decided to seek a restaurant for lunch. After lunch, my mother and I were on the move again, this time to try and find a flat to rent. We did not have immediate success and as we were extremely tired, we sat down at a shelter on the sea front and waited for the time we could arrive back at our digs to have an evening meal. We lived in hope that the next day would bring better luck as far as house hunting was concerned.

Not only did we have the task of trying to find somewhere permanent to live, but I was also faced with the task of finding a job. When I signed on at the Exchange they didn't have a suitable job available. Our landlady, who had once been a secretary at Saunders-Roe (or Westland Aircraft as they were later known), suggested that I send a speculative enquiry to them. To my surprise they invited me for an interview and I began work as a secretary at Westland Aircraft, East Cowes. I started to travel on the bus from Ryde to Cowes, and found myself working in offices adjacent to Osborne House, the country retreat for Queen Victoria that had been built in 1845.

After my mother and I had resided at the guesthouse for a couple of months, my mother found us a flat in Dover Street. The flat was on the first floor of what had once been a vicarage. Our new flat was very pleasant both inside and out. It was very restful to look out the windows onto the grounds and to see the trees and numerous birds. We felt we could settle there quite happily for a while.

The Isle of Wight proved to be a picturesque island, worth exploring. I believe its scenery had offered inspiration to many poets, artists and writers. Although the presence of Queen Victoria at Osborne House in Cowes had affected the growth of Ryde, its initial development could be attributed to the Player family. At the beginning of the eighteenth century they acquired part of the manor of Ashey and began to lay it out in building plots. Prior to that, Ryde consisted mainly of fishermen and mariners cottages and grew from a population of 600 inhabitants in 1795 to 23,000 today. The passenger pier was constructed in approximately 1813, and two years later a regular ferry service between Ryde and Portsmouth began. Many family mansions began to spring up in the 1840s, rather like the one we lived in. Shops, hotels and churches were added to the scene.

After my father had been serving on Beachy Head lighthouse while my mother and I had been living in Ryde for approximately ten months, my father received instructions from Trinity House to make preparations for a transfer to St Mary's lighthouse in Northumberland, our wartime home. My mother and I were sad about the thought of having to move again, the only consolation being that my father would be living at home all the time, instead of spending two months on a rock lighthouse, and it would be a chance for us to meet up once again with some of our friends and acquaintances who were still residing in the North East.

However, I was still working at Westland Aircraft in Cowes and was rather reluctant to leave especially as I enjoyed working there and I had made so many friends. I liked St Mary's Island but I remembered how the tides had caused me so many problems during the war years. I had been prevented from attending school on a regular basis. Now, the tides would stop me from getting to work. I couldn't imagine a boss accepting the tides as a regular excuse for turning up late, or even worse, not turning up at all. It occurred to me that I would have to get my own flat to live in. Faced with this situation anyway I made the tough decision to stay on the Isle of Wight where I had a job and friends. It occurred to me that if it was a failure I could always follow my parents up to Northumberland. My parents moved to St Mary's Lighthouse on 30th May 1960.

About the same time as my parents left Ryde, I met David, my husband-to-be. In September 1960, we went up to stay with my parents, buying an engagement ring in Newcastle-upon-Tyne on the way as we had decided to get engaged on St Mary's Island. We decided to get married on New Years Eve.

I travelled to St Mary's Lighthouse a week before the wedding. Newspaper reporters interviewed me, and I had my photograph taken wearing a sou'wester and oilskin as they thought Grace Darling would have. David and his family arrived at the hotel in Whitley Bay where the wedding reception was to be held. The weather had been rough for several days and we were keeping our fingers crossed. After all the excitement I found it difficult to sleep. I looked out into the dark and watched the beam of light spreading its way across the water as a warning to all those who go out to sea, warning them of the danger of the rocks below. Memories of my childhood at St Mary's came flooding back to me.

Crossing the causeway from St Mary's on the way to the church at Seaton Delaval.
Photograph courtesy of Newcastle Chronicle and Journal Ltd.

On the day of my wedding, newspaper reporters knocked on the door at 8 o'clock in the morning asking me to pose in a boat in my bridal gown. "No", said my mother firmly, "We are rather busy at present". My mother left the house at approximately 11:15, leaving my father and I on our own. He was very protective towards me, at the same time conveying his silent good wishes and approval. When we emerged from the lighthouse to walk out towards the causeway, the newsmen and television cameramen ran towards us with enthusiasm. They ran either side of us, taking photographs all the time. The sun was shining as my father and I walked across the causeway before it was washed over by the tide.

Epilogue

My late father Harold Owen Hall entered the service of the Corporation of Trinity House of Deptford Strond on 23rd May 1922 and retired, accompanied by my late mother, Josephine Mary Hall, from St Mary's Island lighthouse on 5th September 1966. Upon his retirement he was proud to receive a certificate signed by the Secretary stating, "This Certificate is issued as a mark of the Elder Brethren's appreciation of many years of faithful service rendered". Several years after his retirement, automation of Trinity House lighthouses took place and as a result there are now no keepers in continuous attendance.

Memories of my life as a lighthouse keeper's daughter will remain with me forever and I am now glad to be living back by the sea again after many years of my married life living inland in Hertfordshire. For some time now I have been a shoreline member of the Royal National Lifeboat Institution and am now a Governor. Although I no longer live in Northumberland, I am a member of Friends of St Mary's Island. My husband David and I have recently joined the Association of Lighthouse Keepers, and attend their annual general meetings held at Trinity House in London. I had heard my parents talk about Trinity House on so many occasions that it was a pleasure for me to visit the building. We are now also members of the World Lighthouse Society, after a trip to Holland with the Association of Lighthouse Keepers.

I shall never cease to admire the work carried out by men and women past and present who have helped to save lives at sea. We have a lot to thank them for.

My parents at St Mary's lighthouse just before Harold's retirement.
Photograph courtesy of Whitley Bay Guardian and Seaside Chronicle.